2/09C=6
LA=7/05

GÜNTHER BINDING

SERIES EDITOR: HENRI STIERLIN
PHOTOS: UWE DETTMAR

HIGH GOTHIC

THE AGE OF THE GREAT CATHEDRALS

TASCHEN

KÖLN LONDON MADRID NEW YORK PARIS TOKYO

Page 3

Cathedral of Amiens

The rose window in the south transept of the cathedral (1250–1264) has a central six-lobed foil from which radiates a network of filigree tracery. The stained glass with its figural representations (in the middle is a depiction of Christ enthroned) bathes the interior in a constantly changing play of coloured light (see also page 113).

Page 5

Temple of Solomon and the Church of Christ

A miniature from a French *Bible-Moralisée* manuscript, second quarter of the 13th century, Vienna, Österreichische Nationalbibliothek, Cod. 2554, fol. 50v.

© 1999 Benedikt Taschen Verlag GmbH
Hohenzollernring 53, D-50672 Köln

Editor-in-chief: Angelika Taschen, Cologne
Edited by Caroline Keller, Susanne Klinkhamels, Cologne
Co-edited by Christiane Wagner, Stuttgart
Design and Layout: Marion Hauff, Milan
English translation: Ingrid Taylor, Munich

Printed in Spain
ISBN 3-8228-7055-2

Contents

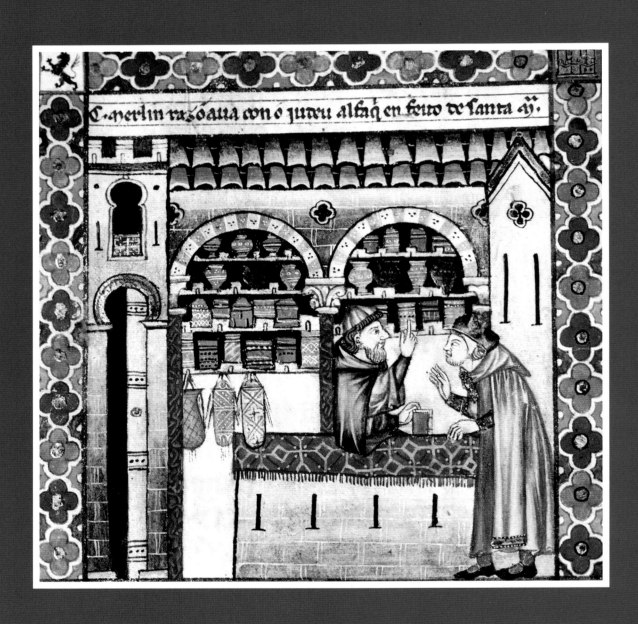

INTRODUCTION

A New Style Emerges from a Changing World

Spanish manuscript from the mid-13th century

Spanish manuscript from the mid-13th century

The codex from which this manuscript comes was originally in the possession of the Castilian king Alfonso X, the Wise (1254–1284). The *Cantigas de Santa Maria* in the library of the Escorial near Madrid contains 1264 miniatures; six images per page tell a kind of picture story. This miniature shows a rich Christian consulting a Jewish apothecary. The furniture in the apothecary's shop, recognisable by the crucibles and containers on the shelves, is integrated into an arcaded architectural style, the details of which are influenced by the Mudéjar style, the style of the Spanish Moors.

For over 200 years architects, art-lovers and researchers from all over Europe and further afield have sought to uncover the secret of Gothic cathedrals, of their forms and power, to develop an understanding of the Gothic era, to bring out its special qualities and to formulate its charm and atmosphere in words. Every one of them believes he or she has reached that goal, or at least is on the right road, one or two steps further along the way towards capturing and explaining the spirit of that style. I am becoming more and more convinced, however, that our ability to appreciate fully the ingenuity of the master builders of Gothic cathedrals is severely impaired, for all too much information and knowledge are still lacking. Yet we must continue to pursue our goal.

This book is neither a scientific anthology nor a psychoanalytic study; it is the work of an architect interested in the structural, formal, historical and religious aspects of Gothic architecture, someone who for years has been enthusiastically attempting to bring the phenomenon of this architecture closer to his students and readers, and to impart to them impressions, knowledge and understanding of this remarkable style.

It is not the intention of this book to present a comprehensive survey of the buildings from the Early and High Gothic periods (1140–1300) – this is extensively treated in other excellent works on individual countries or buildings. The aim is rather to give an overview of the development and the appearance of the style we term 'Gothic'. We take a look at the historical, sociological, theological and technical conditions and the rules of form and design, and we inquire into the significance of the building forms, that is, the representational intention of churches and secular architecture. The most typical demonstration of this is to be found in French cathedral architecture, to which we will therefore devote more space than to the development in England, Germany, Spain and Italy where Gothic architecture began to develop at a later date.

It is hoped that the reader will thereby gain a better understanding of Gothic architecture and learn to appreciate more this immensely impressive style. He or she will gain insight into how people in those days thought and planned, how they designed, organised and built these structures; will learn about the forms they chose and how they developed them; and will examine the 'spirit of the Gothic' which is so clearly legible in the form and structure of the buildings and which is the moving force behind development and form-finding. The written sources are not numerous, but, correctly interpreted, they give good indications and supplement what can still be observed in the buildings which have been handed down to us. Indeed, the Gothic style was not the product of the scholastic theology and philosophy taught at the cathedral school of Chartres, at Saint-Victor monastery in Paris or in the early days of the first university of Paris, in around 1200 (and also being taught at Bologna, Oxford and Cambridge); it resulted instead from political, ecclesiastical and economic developments combining with scholastic ideas to create a situation which also extended to cover architecture. The period of

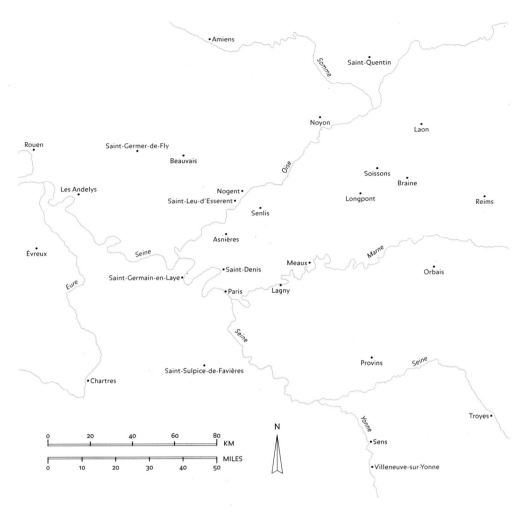

Churches and monasteries in the
Île-de-France around the royal
seat in Paris

Map showing the location of the
most important Gothic buildings
in Europe

the 12th and 13th centuries was a time of intellectual, economic and technical emergence.

No matter how beautiful a photograph, it can be no substitute for experiencing the architecture at first-hand. It can only serve to inspire us to visit the building itself, to take a close look at it and thereby come to understand its impact. A cathedral is like a hefty book, but a book we must first know how to read. The following texts will, I hope, provide you with this inspiration and with some information.

How the Gothic Style Spread

The Gothic style developed far from the cradles of classical architecture, the Mediterranean centres of Athens, Rome and Byzantium. It is not a further progression or transfer of these ancient traditions, arising instead from the buildings and forms of Romanesque churches, and it emerged in France, mostly in the fertile Île-de-France around the residence of the French king in Paris. The first flowering of the Gothic took place under Abbot Suger in the Benedictine abbey church of Saint-Denis (1130/1135–1144), the burial place of many French monarchs, and after the middle of the 12th century in the cathedrals of Noyon, Senlis, Laon and Paris. By the beginning of the 13th century Gothic architecture had reached its mature form in the cathedrals of Chartres, Reims, Amiens (nave) and Bourges,

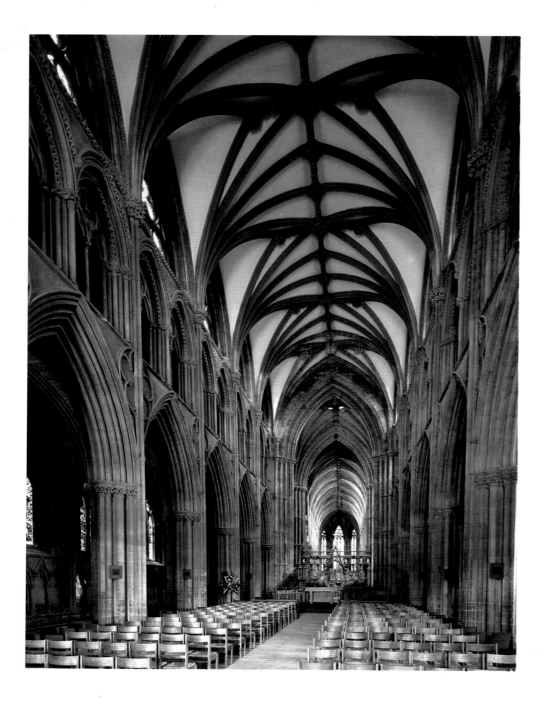

Nave of Lichfield cathedral
Following severe damage in the
17th century, the cathedral of
Lichfield was extensively restored
from 1788 onwards. The interior
and the west front, however, still
give a strong impression of how
the cathedral originally looked in
the 13th century when it was built.
In the second half of the 13th century the triple-aisled, seven-bay
nave was added to the choir and
transept, which date from the first
half of that century (windows and
vault around 1300). A triforium
above the richly profiled arcades
gives rhythm to the wall elevation.
A star vault spans the central nave,
but the aisles have simpler cross-
rib vaults with axial ribs and
keystones.

attaining perfection in the conversion of the abbey church of Saint-Denis from 1231,
in the royal palace chapel of the Sainte-Chapelle in Paris, in the cathedral of Troyes
and in the royal castle chapel of Saint-Germain-en-Laye.

Other countries in Europe gradually began to adopt the body of Gothic forms, as
a result of the influence from developments in France. Laon and Chartres were the
first to have a wider influence, followed more significantly by Reims and the east
sections of Amiens; the construction techniques and style, well developed from
around 1180, spread first to England (Canterbury, Wells, Salisbury, Lincoln,
Westminster Abbey and Lichfield), then, from around 1235, to Germany (Marburg,
Trier, Cologne; Strasbourg and Regensburg from 1275), and to Spain (Burgos,
Toledo). The rigidly organised Cistercian order in Burgundy, founded in 1098, also
contributed to the rapid spread of the Gothic. Examples here are the monasteries
of Royaumont, Longpont (Aisne), Maulbronn and Altenberg.

Our image of the Gothic is strongly determined by the large cathedral buildings
and Cistercian monastery churches, by chapterhouses and refectories, but we must
not forget also that at this time town walls and their impressive gates were being

Page 13
West façade of Lichfield cathedral
Tracery work covers the entire
surface of the mighty west front
which dominates the whole building. This work and the towers
themselves were commenced
after 1280. The crossing tower,
seen here in the background, was
also rebuilt in the 17th century,
along with the spires on the west
towers.

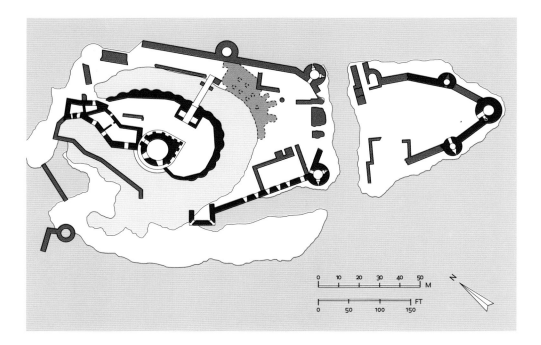

Château-Gaillard near Les Andelys
Upon his return from the Crusades Richard the Lionheart, King of England and also Duke of Normandy, granted a sum of £55 000 from the royal coffers to build the fortress of Château-Gaillard near Les Andelys. Perched high on a 100-metre chalk cliff above a bend in the Seine between Rouen and Paris, the fortifications also encompassed a barrier across the river. Built in just 14 months between 1196 and 1197, the fortress was traditional in form, with a hilltop castle and huge keep. This seemingly impenetrable structure was captured by trickery in 1204, by the troops of Philippe II Auguste, King of France.

extended and new fortresses built. In just over a year, 1196–1197, Richard the Lionheart erected the fortification of Château-Gaillard as a bulwark against the French crown land, at a cost of over £55 000. In 1240 Frederick II erected the hunting lodge of Castel del Monte in the lonely hills of Apulia and several other castles typical of the style such as in Augusta (1239–1242) and Catania (c. 1239) in Sicily. Townspeople were also beginning to build more and more houses in stone; indeed, the oldest half-timbered structures still in existence date from this time, the 13th century, bearing impressive witness to the skills of their builders. In around 1190 the city of Paris had its main streets paved with stone.

The term 'Gothic' conjures up a generally accepted idea of something immutable, unchanged, suddenly complete in form, quite different from the Late Gothic, the Flamboyant style in France, the Perpendicular style in England or Parler architecture in Germany. Yet even the cathedrals of Chartres, Reims and Amiens – generally named as archetypal examples of Gothic architecture – are quite different from each other, and indeed the churches themselves underwent a constant process of change. There are also great differences to be observed between the individual countries and landscapes. The variety and the differing developments are not so much explained by a change of ruler or allegiance to a particular house, but are rooted more in general economic and spiritual phenomena, chance events and personal connections.

The catastrophic fires in the cathedrals of Chartres in 1194, of Reims in 1210 and of Amiens in 1218 were thus to prompt the development of new architectural forms. It was not the arrival of Louis IX, known as Saint Louis, in 1226 that marked the high point of French Gothic – this was instead the rebuilding of the abbey church with the royal tombs at Saint-Denis from 1231, which led to the first pierced triforium, with openings in the exterior wall, and the acquisition of Christ's Crown of Thorns in 1239, which prompted the building of the Sainte-Chapelle as a glass shrine. It was not the King of Germany and Holy Roman Emperor, the Sicilian Frederick II, who promoted the new Gothic style in Germany, but the collegiate churches such as the Liebfrauenkirche in Trier, the Elisabeth church in Marburg, built from 1235 onwards by the Teutonic Order of Knights, and Cologne cathedral that first introduced the French forms. Nor did the Gothic style reach England via Richard the Lionheart, but instead after 1175, through the monks of Canterbury, once again prompted by a devastating church fire.

Above and below

Border fortress on the Seine

View of the hilltop border fortress of King Richard overlooking the Seine valley. The impenetrable, thick-walled keep of Château-Gaillard (1196–1197) is surrounded by a high fortified wall with round towers.

Political Background

Great changes were taking place in political spheres in the 12th and 13th centuries. Frederick II, who lived far from Germany in Italy, tried to unite the empire which had dissolved into strife and decline after the death of Frederick I, Barbarossa and his son and heir Henry VI († 1197). Despite his efforts, the Holy Roman Empire disintegrated after his death into territorial principalities and the towns became more and more independent, gaining at the same time in economic, political and cultural significance. It was not until 1273 that imperial power was reinstated, under Rudolf von Habsburg, but the seven Electors and the free cities retained their independence and their influence on imperial politics.

Developments in France were quite different. There the Capetians had taken over from the Carolingians as rulers in 987 and they gradually brought the small states together into one empire. The Capetians ruled until 1328 from the Île-de-France and, as their imperial influence spread, they of course came into conflict with England under Richard the Lionheart (1189–1199), for England ruled over an important part of the French mainland – Normandy – as well as controlling other extensive French territories. After his return from the Crusades Richard the Lionheart strengthened his Norman fortifications in 1196/1197 by building Château-Gaillard on the Seine between Rouen and Paris, to control the territory around the river. Richard's father, Henry II, who already held Anjou and Maine, had married Eleanor of Aquitaine in 1152, thereby gaining control of Poitou, the Auvergne and parts of Aquitaine. The French king was thus restricted to Toulouse, the western part of Burgundy, Champagne, Vermandois, Flanders and the Île-de-France. Not until 1259, under Henry III, was a peace treaty signed in Paris. But soon after, in 1337, the Hundred Years' War broke out as a result of Edward III of England's hereditary

Pages 16 and 17
Notre-Dame, Paris
On the Île de la Cité in the Seine stood the palace of the French king and the cathedral of the bishop. This richly articulated, linear cathedral lies on the most important transport route in Paris, the river; its dominant west front faces the royal palace. Begun around 1163, the choir was completed, but for the vault, in 1177 and consecrated in 1182. The east section of the nave was built from around 1175 to shortly after 1196. Work began on the twin-towered westwork and the west section of the nave around 1215, with the towers being completed around 1220/1225. Immediately after this the chapels were added to the choir and aisles and the clerestory windows enlarged. From 1258 the south transept front was built under the direction of Pierre de Montreuil.

claim to the French throne through his Capet mother following the end of the Capetian dynasty in 1328.

Since the 10th century the French kings had created a fortified residence on the island in the Seine. Their riches came from the surrounding crown land, the Île-de-France, a very fertile region. No monarchs in Christendom enjoyed more prestige or more riches at the beginning of the 13th century than Philippe II Auguste and his successor Louis IX, who was canonised in 1297. In a characteristic and unusually intensive way the secular was combined with the profane, the temporal with the eternal, to form a single glorious unity, visibly expressed in the cathedrals, monasteries and churches. Still today this is to be seen in the cathedral of Notre-Dame in Paris, the royal coronation cathedral of Notre-Dame in Reims, the abbey

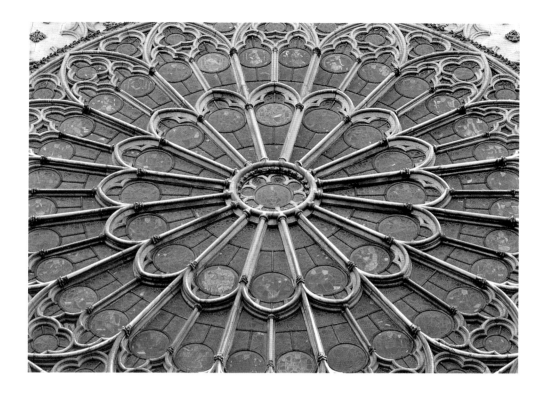

Above and below

The rose windows of Notre-Dame, Paris

The roses of the north and south transepts of Paris cathedral, which were constructed around 1245–1258 and after 1258, show the mature development of the rose window, with openwork corner spandrels (see also page 18). This style had been introduced around 1230 in the north transept of Chartres. The 16-part rose designed by Jean de Chelles on the north transept has an unusual diameter of 13 m, and the division of the lancets into two rows is also rare.

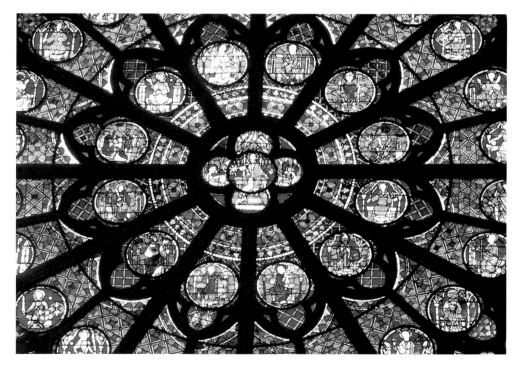

church of Saint-Denis with the royal tombs, the Sainte-Chapelle in the king's palace on the Île de la Cité, in the pilgrimage cathedral of Notre-Dame in Chartres as the most important church in the area dedicated to Our Lady, and in the cathedral of Amiens in what was then the country's richest commercial centre.

The basis for these achievements was a firmly based, ordered social hierarchy, which flourished in France in the period 1140–1280. The same foundation existed in England. In Germany, however, developments took an altogether different path, because the rulers lived in southern Italy and power was divided and fought over between the various secular lords, bishops and cities seeking independence. This was the arena for the tensions arising from the growth of agricultural production on the one hand and the increasing success of commerce on the other.

Intellectual Background

To these changes taking place in society were added the conflicts between popes
and emperors, between kings and the Church, and the beginnings of conflict
between orthodox beliefs and heresy. All this prompted a revision and reorganisa-
tion of Christian teaching on the basis of ancient texts, particularly those of
Aristotle and Plato, which included questions about the nature of being. The result
was an exceptional widening of knowledge in a range of fields, and the Crusades
were one component in this development.

Since 1095 the Crusades had had a substantial and immediate effect on Church
politics and on rulers, above all on their knights, but by 1291, with the fall of Acre,
the last French bastion in the Holy Land, their influence was finally over. At the same
time, around 1300, there was an end to the steady rise in population which had been
experienced for the previous two to three centuries. Epidemics, catastrophes and
war created a setback to this trend. Although this did not lead to a decline in artist c
activity, the emphasis shifted instead to the towns, which had become rich by trade,
and to their citizens.

During this time of great intellectual upheaval the monumental churches, with
their entrance façades guarded by towers, their stone solidity and their rich,
colourful decorations, were a sign of safety, of protection and security. They
pronounced the might of the Eternal, they were the cities of God: their foundations
were Christ, their columns the Apostles and prophets; their stones were the 'living
stones', the community of the believers. Here ruled the traditional order and
security with the promise of the future as represented in the liturgy, visible in the
colour and the light that comes from God.

Theologians in the 13th century developed a comprehensive image of the
creation and of humanity, as well as theories on absolution; through the observance
of religious rites, through good deeds and with money it was possible to buy oneself
freedom from divine punishment for sin, primarily by founding monasteries and
building churches. Even in the 12th century great religious fervour was behind the
success of calls to the Crusades, in particular the calls from the Cistercian abbot
Bernard of Clairvaux (c. 1090–1153), who was able in 1147 to persuade Conrad III of

View of the choir of Saint-Remi, Reims

The choir of the abbey church of Saint-Remi in Reims was built on to the 11th-century nave after 1165/1170. When the patron of building works, Abbot Pierre de Celle, moved to Chartres in 1181, the choir was unfinished. The vault was not completed until around 1200, and it was in this period that the smooth flying buttresses were built. These are among the earliest examples of flying buttresses, a key feature of Gothic cathedrals.

Germany and Louis VII of France to go on a Crusade to the Holy Land to free it from the so-called infidels. In 1189, Frederick Barbarossa and Richard the Lionheart went on the Crusades, followed by Frederick II in 1228 and Louis IX in 1248 and 1270. The Church also put forward the notion that building churches or participating in their construction was as highly regarded in the eyes of God as taking part in a Crusade.

The founding of the Cistercian order in 1098 in Cîteaux led Bernard, who had been the first abbot of Clairvaux from 1115, into the upper echelons of centrally and hierarchically organised power, wielding influence across a broad spectrum in Europe. In around 1150 there were more than 350 monasteries in the whole of the Western world, and during the 13th century 200 new ones were founded.

The Cistercians took a stance in opposition to the Cluniacs (favoured by the nobility) and their sumptuous abbey at Cluny, and against the pomp of the bishops and their buildings. They preached simplicity, and this was clearly reflected in their building practices, in their habit of erecting monasteries in isolated spots far from towns and in their emphasis on craftwork. This coincided with a period of rising prosperity in agriculture; as a result the order flourished. It also gained influence at the royal courts, not only in France, where it was favoured particularly by Blanche of Castile since she had become regent for the young King Louis IX in 1226, but also at the Sicilian court of the Holy Roman Emperor, Frederick II. Louis IX, Saint Louis, also preferred the Cistercian monastery in Royaumont, founded by his father Louis VIII in 1226, as a burial place for his nearest kin. And the Counts of Berg chose as their resting place the Cistercian monastery of Altenberg near Cologne, which they had founded at the site of their family seat. During the course of the 13th century mendicant orders as well as other communities began to establish themselves – the Dominicans in 1216, the Franciscans in 1223. In the towns, which were becoming more and more wealthy, they had great influence and usurped the Cistercians as spiritual leaders.

With Pope Innocent III in 1198 the high point of medieval papal rule was reached. At the Lateran synod in 1215 a whole range of measures was introduced. Church reforms were demanded, and a harsher line against heresy. The foundation of new

orders was restricted and the independence of monasteries and bishops from secular powers upheld, freeing them from the obligation to pay duties. The teaching of transubstantiation was also laid down, which stated that bread and wine in the sacrifice of the Mass really did become transformed into the Body and Blood of Christ. This desire for change and modernisation affected the imagery used in the windows and sculptures in the cathedrals. The close relations between the French king and the pope led finally, under Pope Clement V, previously Archbishop of Bordeaux, to a change in the seat of the Papacy, the pope no longer residing in Rome, but 1309–1377 in Avignon, where he was entirely dependent on the French king.

The period between 1140 and 1260 was a time of great intellectual activity, of the study of Creation, the beginnings of natural science, and of the development of organisational structures, but it was also a period which experienced a blossoming of secular culture, courtly lyrics, the world of the *Minnesänger* and troubadours, of fine living, of *joie de vivre* and pleasure. It was a time of great contrasts, nevertheless

Romanesque-Gothic nave
Church of the Benedictine abbey of Saint-Remi in Reims. The nave with galleries above the aisles dates from the 11th century, the open choir from around 1170–1200. Bishop Remigius, who lies buried here, anointed the King of the Franks, Chlodwig; the ampulla of anointing oil he received from Heaven was used in the Middle Ages to dispense the sacrament in the coronation ceremony for French kings in the cathedral of Reims.

Round pier with capital
In the abbey church of Saint-Remi in Reims the round piers between choir and ambulatory which support richly profiled arcade arches are composed of solid masonry drums topped with bell capitals and foliate decoration.

bound into an overriding spiritual order, which at least partially mirrored the political and social power structures.

The supranatural truth of a world created by God was unassailed in philosophy and theology, and the theologians educated in the cathedral schools, monasteries and universities needed to do no more than recognise the truth, understand it and bring it closer to the ordinary people. The world was broken down into formulae and described. The cathedral with its imagery, in both painting and sculpture, played its part in this view and formed a part of the liturgy.

A parallel development taking place in the 12th and 13th centuries was the rise of chivalric and courtly culture among the nobility and the knights. This brought forth the first universal lay culture in Europe, with attitudes and ideals which also found acceptance among the people of the towns. In around 1270/1280 the second part of the *Roman de la Rose* was written, and after 1307, Dante's *Divina Commedia*. Written in the language of the people, these works were accessible to a wide section of the population.

Economic Background

The 12th and 13th centuries saw the breakdown of the manorial system of the king and of the religious and secular lords – a system extended and consolidated in the 9th to 11th centuries by the Carolingians. The economic and social order altered as the system of socage declined. The continued rapid expansion of the amount of land under cultivation and the rise of urban culture were accompanied by improvements in technology: advances such as iron horseshoes and tackle for working horses, the ploughshare, the scythe, the farm cart and water- and windmills led to higher yields in agriculture. At the same time a three-field system of crop rotation developed which eventually was organised on a village-wide basis, with all farmers rotating in the same rhythm between winter grain, summer grain and fallow. In this way grain harvests were doubled and ploughing, sowing and harvesting were distributed evenly across the whole year. This system also offset the danger of failed harvests.

The warmer climate in the 12th and 13th centuries and the increase in agricultural production created better supplies for the towns, where the population had doubled and where the absence of famine and epidemics had enabled division of labour to be introduced and a craft industry to flourish. This was supported, or perhaps it would be more accurate to say it was made possible, by the consolidation of a money economy, which in turn boosted the growth of trade and crafts.

Royal Palace Chapel, Paris
View of the royal palace with the Sainte-Chapelle in the background, pictured in a scene for the month of June in the prayerbook of John Duc de Berry (1340–1416), *Les très riches heures,* from the Musée Condé in Chantilly. John was the third son of John the Good (1316–1364), later King of France; it is therefore not surprising that the palace of the French kings should have been depicted for him in this illustration, drawn between 1410 and 1416.

Left and right

The splendid Cistercian abbey church at Ourscamp

The Cistercian abbey church of Ourscamp on the Oise, in the diocese of Noyon, was founded in 1129 by Bishop Simon de Vermandois as a subsidiary abbey to Clairvaux. It served as the burial place of the bishops of Noyon. It was consecrated in 1201; a new choir was built here in around 1240–1255 following the forms of the choir at Saint-Denis, where the French kings were buried. The church's function as a bishops' resting place explains the elaborate wall articulation and the rich tracery.

By the middle of the 12th century life for many was either one of urban comfort and wealth or a modest, hard-working existence in the countryside. This fundamental structural change and the prosperity brought by ever more, and ever more extensive, building projects, in conjunction with an increase in the price of labour, led in the first half of the 13th century to a range of innovations. In around 1230/1250 the first scale plans began to appear, and building components began to be systematised and standardised. This again fuelled the production of dressed stone blocks and building components in series. And it paved the way for the geometric tracery designs which developed from 1215 onwards.

Also introduced was a system of buttressing the building frame and, after the middle of the 13th century, a type of building crane with pulley system. All these inventions were emerging at the time the great Gothic cathedrals and the collegiate and monastery churches were being built, most notably those of the Cistercian order with its centralised organisation.

Divine Order Reflected in Stone

Gothic Cathedrals – Art and Symbolism

Page 27

Notre-Dame-en-Vaux, Châlons-sur-Marne

The wheel window on the west façade (c. 1200) of the former collegiate and pilgrimage church of Notre-Dame-en-Vaux in Châlons-sur-Marne is a precursor of the tracery window, evidenced in the spoke-like arrangement of colonnettes (see also pages 108 and 109).

God measures the world

The God of Creation measures the world with dividers, a characteristic tool of the master builder. This sheet from a *Bible Moralisée* dates from the second quarter of the 13th century, and probably came from Reims. It is now kept in the collections of the Österreichische Nationalbibliothek in Vienna (Cod. 2554, fol 1ᵛ).

The Emergence of the Term 'Gothic'

A Gothic cathedral clearly differs from a Romanesque cathedral in many ways. The pointed arch replaced the round arch, the main part of the church was optically narrower and the transept and choir were linked together to form one space instead of two interlinked spaces. The square-based system was overcome by means of rectangular vaults. A system of buttressing the building's frame broke up the massiveness of the walls. Space-enclosing, light-admitting walls replaced thick walls with slit windows, and a grid of tracery took the place of articulated, graduated and niched wall surfaces. The external appearance was no longer characterised by smooth masonry, but was broken up through devices such as buttressed piers, flying buttresses, openwork gablets, pinnacles and tabernacles with statues. And finally the big picture windows, admitting coloured light, embodied truth, for colour is only visible through the divine light.

The word 'Gothic' was first used as a rather negative term. In 1440 Laurenzo Valla (1406–1457) distinguished between Gothic and Roman letters (*Codices gothice scriptos*), whereby for him all things Gothic were bad and all bad things were Gothic. The same forms were mentioned by Giorgio Vasari (1511–1574) in 1550, as well as a 'maniera tedesca', notably a 'maniera dei Goti', and he also mentioned that 'questa maniera fu trovata dai Goti'. He used this term to express his contempt for the art of the north, of the Goths. He described their architecture 'as something monstrous and barbaric, far removed from any harmony, and at best to be described as chaos and disorder. Many buildings of this type are now infecting the world. Their portals show relatively slim columns, which are also twisted in a screw-like fashion and are never formed strongly enough as to be able [credibly] to carry a weight, no matter how small. This accursed style of design is accompanied by lots of confusing, small objects [*tabernacolini*], which are to be found on all sides of the building, covering it almost completely, aligned one above the other and each decorated with a number of obelisks [*piramidi*], peaks and leaves. Such fragile-looking structures become even less stable when bundled together in this way; and they seem rather to be made of paper than of stone or marble. It was the Goths, too, who introduced pointed arches and filled the whole of Italy with their accursed designs.' In 1669 Molière in *La Gloire du Val-de-Grâce* spoke of the insipid taste for Gothic decoration and monstrous horrors. In 1681 Filippo Baldinucci in his *Vocabolario toscano dell'Arte del Disegno* (Tuscan Dictionary of the Art of Design) listed the 'Ordine Gottico' in addition to the classical orders.

Art theory in the north of Europe, in particular in France and Germany, was very dependent on Italy and strongly influenced by the writings of Marcus Vitruvius. Accordingly here, too, in the 17th and 18th centuries, as formulated by François Blondel in 1675 in his *Cours d'Architecture,* the 'immensely unbearable manner which was still common even in the days of our fathers, namely Gothic architecture' was generally rejected. The classically educated Blondel disapproved primarily of the barbaric decoration of Gothic buildings, while still recognising that they 'are never-

theless built in accordance with the rules of art and beneath the monstrous heap of their decoration there is yet a certain attractive symmetry'.

Johann Georg Sulzer, in his *Allgemeine Theorie der Schönen Künste* (General Theory of the Fine Arts) of 1778, followed in the tradition of Vasari when he stated, 'This term is used in a variety of ways in the fine arts to indicate barbaric taste; ... it seems to denote an impropriety, a lack of beauty and good proportions in visible forms, and arose as a result of the efforts of the Goths who had settled in Italy to imitate in an unseemly way the ancient works of architecture.' Nowadays these criticisms may be hard to understand, aesthetically and historically, but they did address those qualities which are the essence of the style: the vertical, the illusionistic, the fragile.

In 1760 Anne Robert Jacques Turgot declared in a lecture to the French Academy that the Gothic style represented a step forward from the Greek and Roman styles of architecture. In his three-volume work on English architecture, 1727–1742, Browne Willis also considered Gothic architecture. So, too, did Batty Langley in 1740/1742 and the Parisian Benedictine monk Bernard de Montfaucon in the five volumes of his *Monuments Français,* 1729–1733, as well as Jean Lebeuf in 15 volumes on the buildings in the diocese of Paris, 1754–1758.

Love of architectural detail

The westwork of Strasbourg minster, begun in 1275 under Erwin of
Steinbach, is richly layered and
decorated.

Above: Gallery above the rose window.

Centre: The upper corner of the
rose window opened up in tracery
(after 1295).

Below: Figures under baldachins in
the archivolts of the church portal
(c. 1280).

Page 32 and 33
Strasbourg minster
The minster of Strasbourg, situated on the banks of the Upper Rhine in the territory of the German kings, was strongly influenced by the French Gothic. It represents a pinnacle of development in Gothic architecture, with its light, open buttress system above the aisles of the nave (c. 1240), and the two lower floors of the westwork (1275–c. 1365) with their filigree layered tracery covering the façade like finely woven threads.

In 1772 the 23-year-old Johann Wolfgang Goethe took a stance against the generally accepted negative view of Gothic architecture, using the example of the minster in Strasbourg, in an essay called *Von deutscher Baukunst* (Of German Architecture). The essay first appeared as an anonymous handbill. He attempted to present the Gothic cathedral as a free and great work of art, basing his argument on what constitutes beautiful proportions. 'The harmony of the volumes, the purity of the forms ... fit together even without a relationship of design; for a single perception turned them into a characteristic whole. For this characteristic art is the one true art. When it creates its effect through internal, unified, unique, independent perception, unconcerned, indeed with no knowledge of all else, whether it be born of crude savagery or formed sensitivity, it is whole and alive. The soul then rises all the more to an understanding of the relationships, which are simply beautiful and eternal, to an appreciation of the truth of its main chords whose secrets we can but feel.' The artistic principle dominant in the Gothic style (and equally as valid as that

of classical antiquity) was not the rigorously proportional relationship of each part to the whole, such as governed understanding of proportion in architectural theory post-Vitruvius, but instead an encompassing accord of form mysteriously drawing together all the individual elements. In 1773 Herder printed Goethe's essay, together with one by the Italian Paolo Frisi called *Saggio sopra l'architettura gotica* (Essay on Gothic Architecture) of 1766 in which the latter turns against Italian Renaissance criticism. The reference to nature found in Goethe was taken up in 1802 by François René de Chateaubriand in *Génie du Christianisme*. Finally the Englishman James Hall, taking the aesthetic angle in his *Essay on the Origin of the Gothic Architecture* in 1813, argued that the Gothic style derives from the imagery of the forests and from the supposedly natural life of the 'uncivilised' Celtic and Germanic tribes.

In the context of the emerging appreciation of medieval art at the end of the 18th century, the word Gothic came to be used in a positive sense, by people such as Marc-Antoine Laugier, William Gilpin and later August Wilhelm Schlegel. Like Goethe, but less emotionally, Friedrich von Schlegel in his *Grundzüge der gothischen Baukunst* (Essential Principles of Gothic Architecture), which he wrote in 1804/1805 while journeying on the Rhine with the Boisserée brothers, praised the choir of Cologne cathedral for 'the beauty of its proportions, the imagination, the evenness of delicacy, the lightness despite the size. All is designed and formed and decorated, and ever higher and more mighty forms and decorations rise up from the first and smaller forms.

The essence of Gothic architecture lies therefore in the natural fullness and endlessness of the interior design and of the exterior floral decoration. When marvelling at the size, this is what takes hold of one, what moves one with its mystery, what uplifts one upon perceiving its pleasant, lively impression. Gothic architecture has a meaning and it is of the highest kind.' Schlegel's observation that 'for all the richness of decoration in Gothic buildings there is a rigorous symmetry, a constancy of form and a harmony in the beautiful richness' touches on the fascination we still feel today when confronted with the intermingling of rigid, geometric shapes with curving, natural forms, a blend which is so characteristic of Gothic cathedrals. Johann Sulpiz Boisserée recognised in 1823 that 'painting on glass enabled the architects of the Gothic style, without too much increase in the height, to place windows where they would otherwise have had to have a solid wall. In this way they were able to avoid all unnecessary mass; they were able, as it were, to build transparent walls and give their buildings a wonderful lightness.'

In his *Handbuch der Kunstgeschichte* (Handbook of Art History) in 1842 and in the third volume of his *Geschichte der Baukunst* (History of Architecture) in 1859, Franz Kugler (1808–1858) placed medieval architecture for the first time in the context of overall art history and examined its distinguishing aspects. In Gothic architecture there was above all 'a striving towards light-filled sublimity and a unified articulation of space. Its builders were very much aware of the mystical effect of an architectural space which was needed for the inspiration of the spirit. ... The mystical is woven into the totality of the Gothic building. ... These spaces rise upwards, airily opening themselves up in the upper reaches to the fullness of light streaming in from outside, the roof seems to be held in swaying motion supported atop rising columns, without mass, like a miraculous vision. The secret of this effect which seems to flout the laws of nature lies in a structure put together with great feeling for its meaning. The entire building mass had broken down into a framework of individual parts, between which were placed only lighter infill sections to close it off to the outside. ...

The elements in this technical system [pointed arch, buttress, cross-rib vault] have been seen in Romanesque architecture ever since architects first tried to place a vault on a basilica. In French Romanesque architecture in particular many ways of approaching this problem can be seen. The view is thus expressed that this entire

Light flooding into Strasbourg minster
In around 1240 a new nave was built at Strasbourg minster; the new structure, with pierced triforium and wide, four-panelled tracery windows (1250–1270), the forms of which are repeated in the aisles, was influenced by the architecture at Saint-Denis.

system is none other than the necessary perfection of those attempts, and there is no lack of well-founded technical proof to confirm such a view. But one thing is overlooked in all this: that the end result, seen purely as a triumph of building engineering, would never have come about, were it not for the complete commutation of spiritual striving, or the ideals which underpinned the task, were it not for the yearning for upward movement, for the light, were it not for the desire to create a wonderful effect.' Kugler pointed out that in 'the new system of Gothic architecture the rigidity of the wall almost entirely disappears and in its place there is nothing but much-membered columns and vaults' and that it had 'brought forth as its most important single features rib vaults, buttresses and rib structures'. This was thus the first recognition of the pre-eminence of the formal over the structural in Gothic architecture.

An important, if not the most significant step forward in general understanding of Gothic forms was made by the French architect Eugène Emmanuel Viollet-le-Duc (1814–1879) in his ten-volume *Dictionnaire raisonné de l'architecture française du XIe au XVIe siècle,* 1854–1868. The structural formalism of Gothic architecture was for him a key characteristic and thus he viewed the load-bearing components and the vaults as a central determining factor in the design, like a kind of skeleton construction, very much in tune with the iron building-frames emerging at the time he was writing in the

Choir of the cathedral of Soissons

If the richly articulated choir of Cologne cathedral can be regarded as the pinnacle of development of the openwork buttress system above choir ambulatories, the choir of Soissons cathedral is an important example of its emergence. The choir of the cathedral of Saint-Gervais-et-Protais in Soissons was begun in around 1200 and by 1212 was already complete. Massive, smooth buttresses stepped back above dripstones support, as in Cologne, double flying buttresses which bear on columns projecting from the clerestory wall. The saddleback roofs of the buttresses are topped only with small finials. Soissons and Cologne represent 80 years of development.

Page 36
Choir of Cologne cathedral

Built from 1248 onwards, the choir of Cologne cathedral was very much in the French tradition of architecture. It was modelled on the choir of Amiens cathedral. Above the radiating chapels (with little articulation, as they were once masked by surrounding houses) rise buttresses with doubly pierced flying buttresses (c. 1300); the buttresses are richly decorated with blind tracery and broken up into pinnacles and finials.

mid-19th century. The knowledge gained from restoration work and from efforts to complete those Gothic churches which were left unfinished is being applied to this very day, albeit with a more advanced understanding of structural engineering. Recent research using modern methods of scientific calculation and the work of Pol Abraham and Arthur Kingsley-Porter has called into question the function of the cross rib as a purely structural member; this means that in order to understand Gothic cathedrals it is not enough just to regard them as buildings determined purely by function and structural factors.

Viollet-le-Duc's thinking was, however, very influential. Also worth mentioning in this context are the works of Camille Enlart in 1902, Robert de Lasteyrie in 1926/1927, Marcel Aubert in 1934, Karl-Heinz Clasen in 1930 and above all Georg Dehio and Gustav von Bezold with their still influential work *Die kirchliche Baukunst des Abendlandes* (Church Architecture in the West), 1892–1901. These authors summed up the work of extensive individual investigations, but they did not advance the overall understanding beyond the level attained by Kugler.

Largely overlooked was the fact that a building has a spatial structure, which is determined by its dimensions and proportions and by the way in which these are

Conch of the south transept
and two-storey chapel of
Soissons cathedral
The south conch of the transept of
Soissons cathedral represents the
transition from the Romanesque
to the Gothic; it was begun in 1176
and completed to a unified design
in just a few years. The windows of
the conch ambulatory, those of
the gallery and the staggered windows of the clerestory are characteristic features of these storeys
separated by cornices. The windows are markedly stepped back
into the continuous wall surfaces.

contained; a space is to be understood in a visionary way (Henri Focillon, Jean Bony). It is Hans Jantzen we have to thank for returning, in 1927, to an analysis of Gothic architecture as a whole; he described the principle of form as a 'diaphanous struc- ture', and stated: 'The wall as the demarcation of the interior space of the church cannot be understood without considering the space itself; this is seen as an opti- cal zone which is as it were placed behind the wall.' After Jantzen a number of attempts were made to characterise Gothic cathedrals in words, and their content can be summarised as follows: in relation to the technical construction which is par- ticularly legible in the buttress system, the visible architecture of the cathedral (the supposed load-bearing components such as vaulting shafts and ribs) is an archi- tecture of illusion.

In the last 20 years many comprehensive works and monographs of individual buildings have been published on Gothic architecture. Worth mentioning is Louis Grodecki who wrote the best overview of 'the Gothic' so far available (Strasbourg 1978), in the series *Storia universale dell'architettura* (World History of Architecture); Dieter Kimpel and Robert Suckale with their book on *Die gotische Architektur in Frankreich 1130–1270* (Gothic Architecture in France 1130–1270), 1985; Norbert Nussbaum's *Deutsche Kirchenbaukunst der Gotik* (Church Architecture of the Ger- man Gothic), 1985 and 1994; Günter Kowa's *Architektur der englischen Gotik* (Archi- tecture of the English Gothic), 1990; and others who are named in the bibliography and who each give an excellent, very readable account, with extensive references for further reading.

The centre point of the church: the crossing

The crossing in Soissons cathedral is the point at which choir, transepts and nave meet. Slim vaulting shafts rise in one continuous line up to the small capitals to support the light, graduated crossing arch and the delicate cross-rib vault.

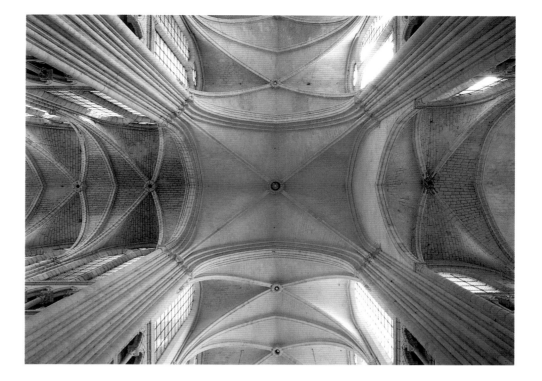

The cathedral of Soissons

The nave of Soissons cathedral, completed around 1230, leads to the older choir with triple-articulated elevation, which was started in around 1200 and finished in 1212. High, slim, distinctly stilted arcades with pointed arches rise from round piers with thin, projecting vaulting shafts; above the arcades is a row triforium; tall, fully opening lancet windows were inserted between the vaulting shafts – at this stage the windows were without tracery, this development being integrated later in the nave and the aisles as plate tracery.

The Symbolism of Cathedrals

The Gothic cathedral is not a manifestation in stone of a particular philosophy, as Erwin Panofsky maintained in his *Gothic Architecture and Scholasticism* in 1948, and Otto von Simson in 1956 in his work *The Gothic Cathedral*, but is imbued with the same spirit as that found in the philosophy and theology of the period. Saint Thomas Aquinas (1224/1225–1274) held that all sciences (*scientiae*) and arts (*artes*) are directed towards the perfection of man, to his happiness (*beatitudo*). According to Hugh of St Victor (c. 1096–1141) man should try, through striving for wisdom (*sapientia*), to recreate the integrity of his nature if he is to find his way back to his true fulfilment in the wisdom of God. Wisdom is the highest form of perfection of reason; it is able to recognise the order which exists between things and which is directed towards a goal. Thus, according to Saint Thomas Aquinas, who took his lead from Aristotle, 'it is the task of the wise to bring about order'.

Quadripartite wall elevation
The south conch of Soissons cathedral, erected in a very short time in 1176, still took up the traditional quadripartite division into arcade, gallery, row triforium and window zone, while later parts of the building have a triple elevation (see page 39). Pillars with projecting shafts alternate with one or two monolithic slim columns which carry the narrow, pointed-arched arcades. Large windows in the ambulatory and in the galleries, and graduated groups of three clerestory windows create a sense of brightness and lightness, distinct from the dark triforium.

Page 41 above
Space topped with light vaulting
At the end of the 13th century in the north transept of Soissons cathedral a tracery rose window with lancet panels was combined with a pierced triforium and the whole topped with light vaulting.

South conch of Soissons cathedral
The shafts supporting the ribs
of the vault extend down to the
sill of the gallery, dissecting
the separate perimeter zone of
gallery, triforium and clerestory.

Every being participates in the divine and beautiful in life, which in medieval understanding was the same as the good. According to Saint Thomas Aquinas, and inspired by the Pseudo-Dionysius, the beautiful adds something in terms of concept to the good: the relationship to knowledge. Alexander of Hales (c. 1185–1245) believed that 'truth is a disposition of form which refers to the innermost being; beauty on the other hand is a disposition of form which refers to the external'. In texts by medieval authors beauty is never spoken of in the sense of 'artistic beauty'. Rather, as mentioned by Hugh of St Victor, 'We are amazed at certain things because they fit together in a clever and harmonious way, so that the very planning of this work seems to a certain extent to indicate the particular attention and care of the founder [of God, *conditor*].' Robert Grosseteste (c. 1175–1253), Bishop of Lincoln, defined beauty even more clearly in 1230: 'Beauty ... is the harmony and accord of a thing within itself and the harmony of all its individual parts within themselves and with reference to the rest and with reference to the whole and it is the harmony of the whole in reference to all parts', and: 'Beauty is the harmony of relationships.' In 1250, in his main work *Summa theologiae,* Saint Thomas Aquinas spoke of beauty in a similar way, but within the context of the teachings of God: 'Three things are necessary for beauty. First completeness or perfection; for incomplete things are ugly. Then the right proportion or harmony. And finally clarity; for we call those things beautiful which have glowing colours.' This is the basis upon which we should evaluate the experience of art in the Middle Ages, particularly in the Gothic era.

Within the teachings of the Seven Liberal Arts (*septem artes liberales*) the four subjects of the quadrivium (arithmetic, geometry, music, astronomy) are concerned with the nature of the world that can be perceived by our senses, on the basis of numbers. They are, however, to be regarded not merely as an end in themselves, as

a means of attaining a better understanding of the world, but also as an opportunity of coming nearer to God and His idea of creation – with the much-quoted clear reference to the statement in the Book of Wisdom (11,21): 'You have ordered everything according to measure, number and weight' (*omnia in mensura, et numero, et pondere disposuisti*). Thus the more a cathedral followed this principle of order fundamental to the cosmos, the more it would be ordered, true and capable of leading the participants in the liturgy to the true understanding, to God, 'who is alone the creator and maker [artist] of nature' (Hugh of St Victor).

Even Plato (427–347 B.C.), in *Philebus,* a work which although unknown in the 12th century nevertheless contained ideas which were familiar, explained, 'If one separates the arts of arithmetic, measuring and weighing from all the arts, then that which remains of each of them is only a small portion. ... I would not describe as beauty of form that which most would probably believe, namely the beauty of living bodies or certain paintings. What I would describe as beautiful is rather something straight or circular, and from these then the surfaces and volumes which are turned or defined through spirit levels or squares, ... for these are always in themselves beautiful and have a unique attraction.' Plato expressed himself in a similar vein in the first half of *Timaios,* which was translated into Latin by Calcidius. According to Saint Augustine (354–430) the equilateral triangle is more beautiful than the nonequilateral triangle because there is more uniformity within it; even more beautiful is the square with equal angles and sides; but most beautiful of all is the circle, in which no angle disturbs the continual uniformity of the whole.

The theoretical ideas of Plato and Saint Augustine were applied practically by the Spaniard Dominicus Gundissalinus (c. 1140/1150): 'Each skilled person in the

Collegiate church of Notre-Dame-en-Vaux, Châlons-sur-Marne
The sequence of construction of the church is clearly seen in this view from the southwest: nave and transepts were built in 1170/1180, and the clerestory and choir after 1187–1217; the twin-towered west façade was built later, around 1220/1240.

Quadripartite wall elevation
The nave of the collegiate church
of Notre-Dame-en-Vaux in Châlons-sur-Marne, built between
1170 and 1200, has the distinctive,
quadripartite wall elevation typical of the Early Gothic: wide arcades open to the aisles, above
them the galleries with double
arcades below discharging arches.
The upper part of the elevation
is sectioned, each section with
a simple triforium below the window zone.

mechanical arts [for example a craftsman, smith or mason] is involved in the practi-cal application of geometry. Through its application he forms lines and surfaces, creating square, round and all kinds of other shapes in the material subject to his skill.' The master craftsman Villard de Honnecourt began a chapter in his handbook (written around 1220/1230) with the words, 'Here begins the art of the [basic] prin-ciples of drawing, as taught in the art of geometry, to facilitate working.' Even Pliny the Elder (A. D. 23–79) told of a painter who was trained in particular in arithmetic and geometry, and who, without these, would have not been able to practise his art.

In addition there are the harmonic theories, based on numbers, by Saint Augus-tine (*De musica,* 387/388), Boethius (c. 480–525), Cassiodorus (first half of the sixth century) and Isidore of Seville († 636) which built on the Pythagorean theories and gained a firm place in school education during the Middle Ages. Cassiodorus stated succinctly, 'The number is that which determines all.' Similarly Isidore of Seville said, 'Take the number out of all things and everything will collapse.' According to Boethius 'everything which has been put together by the original nature seems to have been formed by the logic of numbers'. For Augustine, divine wisdom could be perceived in numbers, 'for all things have forms, because they have numbers'. He saw in this a moral obligation to search for understanding, which 'without a knowl-edge of the meaning of numbers' would not be possible: 'That is the ordering of the striving for wisdom, through which one is capable of understanding the world order.'

Finally, Alanus ab Insulis wrote at the end of the 12th century in the tradition of Augustine, that God, as a 'skilful architect' (*elegans architectus*) or as the 'maker of the universe' (*universalis artifex*) put together the world as his royal palace accord-ing to musical harmonies. Thierry of Chartres († after 1149) said, 'There are thus four kinds of proof [*rationes*] which lead man to a knowledge of the creator: namely the evidence of arithmetic, music, geometry and astronomy. These methodical tools [*instrumenta*] must be used in theology in a shortened form, so that both the [art] work [*artificium*] of the creator is visible in the things, and so that that which we have laid down according to reason is explained.' In the end all these reflections come down to the fundamental concern of the Middle Ages – order [*ordo*].

A knowledge of the meaning of numbers is at the same time a knowledge of the universe. The individual numbers 1, 3, 7, 12, 24 and so on have great significance and symbolise for example, God, the Trinity, the days of Creation, the Apostles and the prophets, the elders, and so on. There were precious few medieval authors who did not expect a revelation of hidden truths from an understanding of number. The authors were distinctly inventive in theological interpretations, and these also had an effect on the number of architectural components, in line with the general belief that 'the built church is an indication of the spiritual church' (*ecclesia materialis significat ecclesiam spiritualem*). Numbers, like geometry, have a part to play in the constant, visible form of a building. It was arithmetic and geometry that enabled medieval man to understand the order of the cosmos, in other words the world, and also to create the built church as an indication of the spiritual one.

An equivalent symbolic value for architects of the Middle Ages came from the buildings described in the Bible, such as Noah's Ark (Genesis 6,14–16), the Taberna-cle of Moses (Exodus 26,1–37; 27,1–21), the Temple of Solomon (I Kings 5,15–32; 6,1–38; 7,13–51; 8,1–8; II Chronicles 3–7), Ezekiel's vision of a new Kingdom of God (Ezekiel 40,1–42,20; 43,13–17) and the New Jerusalem of the Apocalypse (Revela-tion 21,10–21). These were all created according to the will of God. Patristics and the Middle Ages shared the opinion of Quodvultdeus, the Bishop of Carthage (* c. 453), who 'claimed the dimensions of the Ark, the size of the Tabernacle and the height of the Temple of Solomon as typological signs [*figura*]'. From the 8th to the 13th centuries, in the hymns sung at the consecration of a new church, the building was celebrated as an earthly image of the Heavenly Jerusalem, and its component parts

Saint-Denis near Paris
Graduated, pillared portal with figured archivolts. Built on the west side of the abbey church in 1130–1140 by Abbot Suger. The original inscription on the bronze doors commissioned by Abbot Suger, reads:
'Whosoever you may be that wishes to sing the praises of these wonderful doors: glory not at the gold and the costs, but at the work that is in this feat! Noble is the work, but the work which shines here so nobly should lighten the hearts so that, through true lights, they can reach the one true light, where Christ is the true door. What nature this interior is, is determined by the golden door within them. The dull spirit rises up through the material to the truth, and although he was cast down before, he arises new when he has seen this light.'

Porta coeli – door to Heaven
Central portal on the west side
of the Benedictine abbey church
of Saint-Denis. This is the door
through which the king processed
on special feast days, and through
which his body was carried for
burial in the choir. Columns in the
stepped jamb show figured archivolts which supplement the relief
programme on the tympanum.

were placed in parallel with the active members of the Church. Even the Venerable
Bede († 735) and, after him, Amalar of Metz (775/780–c. 850), Sicard of Cremona
(c. 1155–1215) and Durandus of Mende (1230/1231–1296) wrote extensively about
the parallels between the living community and the built church. The Temple of
Solomon is seen as a prefiguration of the Christian Church, which means, accordingly, that the church building is a development of the temple in the same way as
the liturgy of the Church reflects and heightens the temple cult.

Abbot Suger of Saint-Denis also expressed himself in similar vein. The new
church should be an image of the Temple of Solomon, which, we read in the Book of
Wisdom (9,8), was an image of the Tabernacle of Moses, constructed according to
the will of God. Worshippers entering the west portal of Saint-Denis were stepping

Pages 46 and 47
Founded by Pope Urban IV in 1262
The collegiate church of Saint-Urbain in Troyes was founded by Pope Urban IV in 1262 on the site of his parents' house. The choir and transept were sufficiently complete in 1266 for the roof to be put on. The individual forms of the church are influenced by the Sainte-Chapelle in Paris, such as for example the lack of a tripartite wall elevation, and the use of large, double-storey tracery windows in the choir which, above a dark base, transform the walls into luminous glass spaces (comparable to the cathedral in Regensburg, which was built at a later date). On the outside, openwork gablets on the windows rise up between the buttresses to the level of the eaves, where they are topped with a finial.

as it were through the door to Heaven towards the true light, with Christ being the true door. In the liturgical treatment within the built church we can perceive, symbolically, the living Church, the community of the believers. Suger noted in a report on the consecration of his church: 'In the middle 12 columns, which represent the 12 Apostles, in the second row again as many columns in the aisles, representing the number of the prophets, all lifted the building up high, like the Apostle building in a spiritual sense who says: You are now not guests and strangers, but walk with the Saints and are members of the House of God, built on the foundation of the Apostles and prophets, with Jesus Christ himself as its most excellent cornerstone, linking the two walls in which the whole building, both spiritually and physically, grows to become one holy temple in the Lord. The higher and the more befitting we endeavour within it to build in the physical sense, the more we will be taught that we, through our own efforts, are built up spiritually into a house of God in the Holy Spirit.'

In 1286/1296 Durandus of Mende began his extensive work on the liturgy with the sentence: 'Everything which is a part of the church service, the various objects and ornaments [*ornamenta,* that is, the splendid artefacts such as altars, reliquaries,

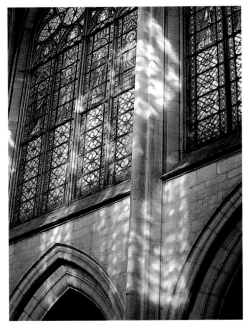

robes, instruments, books], is full of divine signs and secrets.' In a later chapter he stated, 'Indeed the physical church, in which people come together to praise God, indicates the holy church which is built in Heaven from living stones.'

Such typological and allegorical allusions were also presented (following the Venerable Bede in England) by Amalar of Metz, Archbishop of Trier and teacher at the Court School in Aachen, in his book of 823 dedicated to the Emperor Louis the Pious (*Liber officialis*), a work highly regarded throughout the Middle Ages: 'When we come together to pray to God, it is appropriate for us to know that we must have the work of building the walls for our church, like those the city of Jerusalem had. ... The walls of our church are founded in Christ, on his foundation are fixed the Apostles and as they through this believed, so do we believe. We are putting these walls together now, and they will continue to be built up until the end of the world. Each and every one of the Saints whom God has ordained to eternal life is a stone in these walls. One stone is laid on top of the next when the teachers of the church train disciples to study, to teach, to improve, and to strengthen the holy church. Each one has above him a stone that bears a brotherly load. ... The bigger stones, both the smoothed ones and the hewn blocks, which (as an outer skin) are placed in front on both sides, in whose middle the smaller stones lie, are the more perfect men who preserve the weaker pupils or brothers in the holy church through their exhortations and prayers. The walls cannot be strong without mortar, mortar is made from lime, sand and water. The seething lime is the love, which combines with the sand. ... But to make lime and sand suitable for use in building a wall, they have to be mixed with water. Water is the Holy Ghost. ... For in the same way that the stones in a wall cannot be linked together without mortar, nor can people be brought together in the building of the New Jerusalem without the love of the Holy Ghost.'

These comments make it clear to us that theological ideas were not the prime mover in the design of Gothic cathedrals. Such ideas belong firmly in the realms of theoretical knowledge and theological science and they are to be interpreted in the traditional way, as was done from long before the 12th century. The ideas were a conceptual aid in both Romanesque and Gothic cathedrals, but did not determine form.

The Gothic cathedral is not only the place in which the liturgy is practised, but it is also itself a part of that liturgy, with each detail having symbolic or allegorical significance. As such, in a theological interpretation, the cathedral is a construct

Left, centre and right
Collegiate church of Saint-Urbain, Troyes
In the collegiate church of Troyes, built in 1262–1275, the coloured glass in the windows creates a wonderful, ever-changing play of light on the profiled archivolts of the arcade arches, on the mullions of the window tracery and on the walls, already lightened with blind tracery and pinnacles.

Rows of figures under baldachins
On the west portal of Reims cathedral (1255–1285), in front of the deeply stepped jamb, are rows of larger-than-life-size figures under a baldachin frieze.

largely removed from earthly existence; it is a heightened form of the Tabernacle and of the Temple of Solomon, building types which, from ancient times to the contemporary, that is medieval, church, refer to the New Jerusalem of eschatology. The work, as the result of the activities of the architect and master builder, the building which helps us see the Light and feel the beauty of God's Kingdom, provides a fitting setting for the soul's rise from the material to the immaterial world, a place for spiritual exercises, 'through geometric and arithmetical methods' (*geometricis et arithmeticis instrumentis;* Abbot Suger of Saint-Denis). Number and geometry are the forces of order in this world as an indication of the perfect, divine order of the cosmos, whence the divine light comes and is reflected in the glowing colours.

In order to grasp the meaning of a medieval church building, it is necessary first to perceive the theological and philosophical background as the totality of all means to gain knowledge of God, of the transcendent divine being. During the course of the 13th century (beginning first in France – in Chartres and Paris) a general striving was becoming evident, in all areas, to determine the exact place of mankind both in terms of his reason and his nature, within the harmonious, well-proportioned cosmos of creation, in other words in the perfect forms in which God reveals Himself. Efforts were made to understand the secret of the world and to point out the innate divine order within it.

Arithmetic, geometry, music and astronomy were the 'instruments', that is, the methods which even according to Suger were necessary 'so that the work could be brought about more skilfully and laudably'. In the overall context of a primarily theological interpretation of a church building the geometry must be considered as a fundamental design tool in Gothic cathedrals. A Gothic cathedral is determined by 'rationality', such as was expressed by Thierry of Chartres († after 1149, from 1142 Chancellor at Chartres) and Suger of Saint-Denis. According to Plato's *Timaios,* the first half of which was extensively read and studied at Chartres, there had to be a proper reason and principle behind everything that was created. In architecture this is number and geometry, which cause structure and evidence patterns of origin. Thus in the Parisian *Bible-Moralisée* illustrations of 1220/1230, the architect as well as the God of Creation is typically depicted with a pair of dividers in his hand, an instrument through which the architectural work, the product of mental effort (*in mente conceptum*), is turned into lasting reality. These thoughts, in the 12th century,

Choir of Reims cathedral
Rebuilt after a fire in 1211, the choir ambulatory has radiating chapels, very early tracery windows, between which angels stand guard over the church, filigree latticework on the roof parapet and richly decorated buttresses with double flying buttresses (c. 1235/1240).

prepared the ground for the new cathedral which was to be built in the 13th century in the Île-de-France.

The composition of the cathedral was not left to the initiative of the artists, but was instructed by the Church, based on the principles and traditions laid down by theologians in the second council of Nicaea in 787; the 'artist' was entrusted with the technical implementation of the work, on the basis of his experience. No written documentation has been handed down to us to indicate the type of theological brief given to the builder, who by then was being referred to as the *architectus,* taken from the First Letter to the Corinthians (3,10) by the Apostle Paul: 'According to the grace of God which is given unto me, as a wise masterbuilder, I have laid the foundation.' Even the writings of Abbot Suger, which are drawn upon for so much other evidence, give no concrete indications, save for a few general allusions.

With the introduction of the teachings on transubstantiation (see 'Introduction') at the Lateran synod in 1215 under Pope Innocent III there presumably also arose a greater striving to bring out the symbolic function of the building's components. Following early attempts in the sculptural programme on the west front of St Pantaleon, Cologne, around 1000 and in the writing on the columns of St Michael, Hildesheim, in 1015/1022, efforts became concentrated on the portals as a focus of symbolic content. But not until the High Gothic did the architecture of cathedrals really become symbolic to a much greater degree.

In Reims, figures of angels over the buttresses protected the choir in the cathedral; in the Sainte-Chapelle in Paris and in Cologne cathedral, figures of the Apostles drew attention to the significance of the walls and piers upon which they were depicted (12 piers – 12 Apostles). The sculptural programme of the portals covered the entire façade of the church, in Reims also the interior walls. The cycles of glass paintings told the Biblical stories in a variety of ways. The all-pervading symbolism did not even halt at the building forms themselves; but exactly to what extent the symbolism of the building design and forms was laid down from the start, or interpreted at a later stage by educated theologians, can only be decided on a case-by-case basis.

The large number and variety of theological texts led to the need for an overview of them all. This was compiled in the 13th century by, among others, Durandus, Bishop of Mende from 1286, in his *Rationale divinorum officiorum,* a presentation of the entire liturgy, and Vincent of Beauvais (1184/1194–c. 1264), educator and librarian at the court of King Louis IX, with his *Speculum maius,* an encyclopedia of around 2 000 source texts.

A huge number and variety of interpretations of the built church and its components continues to be published. See the Bibliography, especially Joseph Sauer in 1924 with his *Symbolik des Kirchengebäudes* (Symbols of the church); Edgar de Bruyne's *Études d'Esthétique médiévale,* 1946; Günter Bandmann's *Mittelalterliche Architektur als Bedeutungsträger* (Architecture and its symbolism in the Middle Ages); 1951, and finally Günther Binding in 1996 with *Der früh- und hochmittelalterliche Bauherr als sapiens architectus* (The client in the Middle Ages as 'sapiens architectus').

Sainte-Chapelle, Paris

In front of the stained-glass windows of the Sainte-Chapelle (1241–1248) are large statues on brackets under baldachins, an allusion in stone to the Apostles and prophets who hold up the spiritual church, the *ecclesia spiritualis,* in the same way that the pillars support the church building. At the same time the restored painted decoration and the original windows enhance the rich colour effect in the interior.

Stained-Glass Windows –
An Expression of Gothic Metaphysics of Light

In Gothic churches windows became a key element in the spatial design. Up to that point windows had served only as openings in the wall to enable light to enter; they had been mere holes, varying in size, through which light was channelled into the space, illuminating and dividing it in different ways. In Gothic architecture, however, the windows derive their effect from the structure of the spatial divide, this divide being itself a spatial construct and appearing as a source of light. Although in this progression the windows are behind the sculptured elements of the window tracery, the coloured light they transmit gives them, too, a spatial appearance, extending the flat plane of the glass into another dimension. The penetration of the light into space and the luminosity of the glass windows are immediately noticeable.

In the course of development towards the wall structure of the High Gothic, the window surfaces become ever larger as the structure of the stone walls is broken up; thus the significance of the windows is not so much as a part of the wall, more that they come to dominate the entire surface of that wall. Their interaction with the articulated walls diminishes in the same ratio that the glass windows themselves become walls, as can be seen for example in the extensive glass walls at Troyes, Saint-Denis, Cologne, Metz and Strasbourg. The consequence is their integration in the articulation of the wall, the elements of which are continued in the window, thus creating a unified entity in which stone structures also divide the large window surfaces and thus integrate them into the building's structure. A network extending across the whole wall now forms the structure of the spatial divide, with the coloured light from the windows continuing to play an important role.

As laid down by Abbot Suger of Saint-Denis in 1140, light should be a determining element in the design of the interior of a church. He described radiating chapels 'through which the whole church appears in full glory, through the wonderful, never-ending light from the bright glowing glass permeating the beauty of the interior'. In a contemporary manuscript of a *Speculum virginum* in the Cologne city archives, published by Jutta Seyfarth in 1990, a dialogue appears for comparison: 'Have you ever entered a church which is lit by the decoration of stained-glass windows?' Answer: 'You jest with me. This custom is now so prevalent in churches that without it even that which otherwise serves as decoration would be nothing.' The first speaker continues, 'When the rays of the sun now penetrate the coloured glass with their glory, to whom would you then ascribe the colour on the walls? What is it that you see that has penetrated through the pane of glass?' Answer: 'Quite without doubt I ascribe the beauty and colour of the light on the walls to the rays of the sun, not to the glass. ... If it were not for the rays of the sun, the coloured glass could not show what artistry it has captured.'

This understanding of beauty derives from the teachings of Dionysius the Areopagite, also called the Pseudo-Dionysius (c. 550), on the symbolism of light which had a significant influence on medieval thinking. He held that colour had a high level of beauty attributed to it through its substantial association with light; for light is the power which gives colour its character. This concept goes back to Plotin, who claimed there was one simple beauty, namely colour: for colour signifies the victory of light over darkness. God is the light. At the same time, however, according to Robert Grosseteste, light is 'beautiful in itself, because its nature is simple and at the same time contains all within it. For this reason it is to a high degree uniform and extremely harmoniously proportioned through its uniformity. Beauty is a harmony of proportion.' Here the glowing colours of stained-glass windows are superior to painted colour, for they can give beauty a spatial dimension through their coloured light, and thus enhance the reality and effect of the light.

The extensive glass walls in Gothic cathedrals are to be regarded as a link between the sum of new experience in building and neo-Platonic and scholastic metaphysics of light. In the scholastic science of being, light, as the 'first and general form' (*forma prima et communis*), also stands for the 'form of the perfect body' (*forma perfectionis*

corporis); since that which is formed by light is viewed as the real beauty – that in which is also revealed the good or the divine, in the theological sense – it is light that, through its power, lends beauty and sanctity to the material, and thus also to the architecture of a church. As such it is easy to understand the tendency to build ever larger windows in the house of the Lord, the church, to bring more and more fullness of light and therefore divine light into the building, as a presentiment of the Heavenly Church or the time of redemption. Ulrich of Strasbourg († 1277), before whose eyes the nave of Strasbourg cathedral was built, commenced a discourse *On beauty* with the words, 'In the same way that form is the quality of every thing ... so, too, is it the beauty of every thing ... insofar as it through the nobility existing in its form is like the light that streams over the thing which is formed.'

Durandus of Mende saw church windows as 'holy scriptures, which hold off wind and rain, but which admit the light of the true sun, namely God, into the church, in other words into the hearts of the believers, and which bring enlightenment to those within'. What cannot be answered is whether the symbolism of light in the 13th century sank to the level of convention, to be perpetuated only in the institutionalised teaching and thinking of high scholastic circles, without being applied consciously in architecture.

It must be noted, however, that the 'classical', light-and-colour based architecture of the cathedrals of the Île-de-France, and therefore also those in Strasbourg and Cologne, was not a general phenomenon. More common were small-scale windows as openings in the wall, as for example in Freiburg minster, where the builders made use of the forms from Strasbourg, but did not opt for the pierced triforium blending into a single unit with the windows. The same is true of the nave of St Lorenz church in Nuremberg. In this case it is impossible to say what the main influences in its design were – a lack of knowledge or construction skill, or just a more traditional view of spatial arrangement? Also unanswered is why the architects forsook the theologically based, representative approach in favour of decorative and structural forms.

THE GOTHIC BUILDING SITE

Perfect Organisation

Page 57
Construction work
This section of the stained-glass window 'Lazare et le mauvais riche' shows stonemasons at work. The window is in the cathedral of Bourges on the north side of the choir ambulatory. It was created around 1210–1214.

Gothic building site
This page from the *Grandes Chroniques de Saint-Denis* shows work in progress on a Gothic church in the 14th/15th century: On the left stonemasons work on pillar profiles, tracery and dressed stone blocks, on the right a labourer is mixing mortar; the mortar is put in a special carrier and taken up a ladder to the scaffolding where a stonemason lays the blocks; inside is a hoist which is being used to haul up a stone block on a wooden platform. (Toulouse, Bibliothèque municipale, MS 512, fol. 96)

Gothic buildings are above all the legacy of hard-working, enthusiastic organisers, experienced architects, gifted stonemasons and other craftsmen as well as countless labourers. The group of people involved in the building would have consisted of the following: first, the client, theologically trained or a lay person, often wielding great political influence – the one who commissioned the work and who determined the building's purpose (*significatio*). Secondly, a functionary, theologian or lay person, to whom was entrusted, either on a long-term or annual basis, the administration of the building works (*magisterium*). As head of the church masons' guild (*fabrica*) he was also responsible for administering the budget, purchasing materials and invoicing. This function was referred to either as the *magister operis* (master of works) or as *provisor fabricae*. Finally, the third person, also called *magister operis,* but in this case a master builder, a skilled craftsman (*artifex*) who determined technical issues connected with the project (*opus*) and the construction (*structura*). He supervised the work of 'masons, stonemasons, sculptors, carpenters and other workmen' (*caementarii, lathomi, sculptores, carpentarii et alii operarii,* as Abbot Suger of Saint-Denis called them), and of innumerable ordinary labourers.

Building Administrator and Master Builder

There is much evidence for the existence of a respected *magister operis* (the second described above), referred to in German sources during the late Middle Ages as a 'works master' or 'master builder'. As for example in Nuremberg, Augsburg, Constance and Cologne, he was employed by the town council and chosen from among the ranks of the patrician class; he was elected for a period of one year to oversee the construction of buildings commissioned by the council, in particular to manage the finances and monitor the use of public money in these projects. His responsibilities extended to parish churches and even cathedral churches if these served the local people as a parish church, such as was the case in Strasbourg, Freiburg, Regensburg, Vienna and Siena. One such elected overseer of the cathedral factory (also called *fabrica*) in Strasbourg was Konrad Olemann, member of the council and citizen of the town; between 1261 and 1274 he was variously described as *procurator fabricae, appreciator fabricae, magister fabricae, magister seu rector fabricae* and *magister operis*. In the case of Cologne cathedral, a number of titles were used for the administrators of the *fabrica,* that is those people entrusted with administering the funds for building the cathedral and monitoring expenses and income. Original documents give evidence of the following terms for this work, carried out during the time the choir was built between 1248 and 1322: *provisor fabricae, magister seu provisor fabricae, provisor seu rector nove fabricae, magister operis* and *procurator fabricae*.

From the end of the 13th century the terminology became more streamlined as the names *procurator fabricae* and *provisor fabricae* began to be more common as a description of the function of the administrator of the 'factory assets'. In documents concerning St Dunis monastery in Holland in 1265 the first mention of a

'master of this church, called the church master' (*magistri eiusdem ecclesiae, qui dicuntur kercmesters*) is to be found. From the 12th century onwards the sources begin to speak more often of the administrator of the church factory as an *operarius*. Lay administration and management of church building projects seems to have been quite widespread towards the end of the 13th century, as evidenced by the National Council of Würzburg in 1287 which devoted a separate chapter to 'Lay people who administer the church factories' (*De laicis, qui fabricae ecclesiae administrant*).

Between 1276 and 1281, during the construction of the city walls of Koblenz, two administrators of the buildings fund are mentioned: Jacobus clericus, chaplain to the archbishop of Trier at St Castor church in Koblenz, and Wolframus laicus. Between 1284 and 1286 there was only one administrator, the juror Gernot, and in 1288/1289 this function was carried out by the citizen Hildebert. Hildebert himself said of his duties that he was elected by the mayor, the knights, the jurors and other citizens of Koblenz to collect taxes and administer the monies. The buildings fund paid for all costs arising directly or indirectly from the building of the city walls. Every six months the administrator of the fund presented the accounts to a committee of the town council, a body which in 1289 consisted of ten members – three canons from St Florin and St Castor, two knights, two jurors and three citizens. A similar picture emerged in Paris, where in 1190 King Philippe II Auguste engaged seven town jurors on the construction of the city's stone walls and towers. Around the middle of the 13th century the first master builders employed by the towns started to appear in France. In Augsburg in 1320 two 'baumaister' were mentioned. In Nuremberg, at the beginning of the 14th century, historical documents gave evi-

The King at the building site
On the left is King Offa (757–796), seen visiting a building site accompanied by his master builder, identified by his compasses and straight-edge, and the foreman of the site. Two labourers transport stone blocks on a wooden platform up a walkway made of long planks with horizontal bars. Below them a labourer is pushing a barrow. (Matthew Paris, *Life of Saint Alban and Saint Amphibalus,* c. 1250; Dublin, Trinity College, TCD MS 177, fol. 59).

How a cathedral is built
The illustration on the right shows stonemasons, carpenters and labourers at work. On the left of the picture a labourer is using a rope winch to haul mortar in a basket up to the stonemasons working on the wall; the masons check the positioning of the stone blocks using a plumb line and bob. On the right-hand side a stonemason uses a double-headed tool to work a capital, and a carpenter smooths a beam using an axe wielded with two hands. Standing on the ladder is a carpenter who is erecting the scaffolding. (Matthew Paris, *Life of Saint Alban and Saint Amphibalus*, c. 1250; Dublin, Trinity College, TCD MS 177, fol. 60)

dence of the job of 'baumeister' or 'paumeister', engaged by the council to manage the town's building projects.

Our present-day interest in finding out the names of those master builders who created our Romanesque and High Gothic cathedrals, and who possessed such great skills in architecture and design, has prevented a more critical, objective analysis of the sources. Indeed, in some cases this has resulted in some respected local citizen and member of the town council or canon, who acted as buildings administrator, *magister operis, operarius* or *architectus,* being mistakenly interpreted as the master builder who actually carried out the work.

The master builder in charge of the technical side of construction (the third category described above), also called *magister operis,* was a master mason (*magister caementarii*) or master stonemason (*magister lapicidae*) who had gathered experience of working on many large-scale building sites during his journeyman years. This becomes clear from a description by Gervase of Canterbury, who wrote in 1185 about the reconstruction of the cathedral of Canterbury after the devastating fire of 5 September 1174: 'The brothers had now sought advice as to how and in what measure of reason the burned church could be reconstructed, but they did not find it. ... Thus skilled labourers (*artifices*) were summoned from France and England, but even they were not in agreement in the advice they gave. ... One of the labourers was a man from Sens, William by name, a man active and ready, and as a workman most skilful in wood and stone. This man they took, and dismissed the others, because of his gift of lively invention and because of the good reputation in the work.'

Canterbury – the work of a French architect

In 1175 William of Sens was commissioned to rebuild Canterbury cathedral, which had been destroyed by fire. William decided to construct a new building, the first Gothic church in England: round pillars with capitals, vaulting shafts of Purbeck marble and cross-rib vaults.

In September 1178 the scaffolding for the crossing vault collapsed and William fell. Severely injured, he was confined to his bed. 'But because the winter was approaching and it was necessary to complete the upper vault, he entrusted a hard-working and clever monk, in charge of the masons, with the completion of the work. ... The master, however, who was lying in bed, gave orders as to what needed to be done first and what later. In Spring, when the master realised that the physicians were not able to heal him, he gave up his post and returned over the sea to France. Taking over from him as master of works was another William, an Englishman by birth and small in stature, but very skilled and hard-working in many areas.' From this report we can see that the master builder, trained and experienced in working with wood and stone, not only led the building work, but also carried out some of it himself; it also reveals that no construction plans were used, the overall work being instead conceived in the head, as several other sources confirm.

The responsibilities become even clearer in a contract dated 1261, made for the construction of the abbey church of Saint-Gilles-du-Gard in Provence. The agreement was drawn up between on the one side Guillaume de Sieure, abbot of Saint-Gilles, and Valentin de Mirabello, buildings administrator (*operarius*) of the monastery, and on the other master builder (*magister*) Martin de Lonay, inhabitant cf Posquires (Vauvert near Nîmes), in particular about the implementation, the preparation and the organisation of the building of the said church. At the spoken or written behest of the abbot, the buildings administrator (*operarius*) or other person, Master Martin had to present himself at the construction site between the Feast of Saint Michael (29 September) and Whitsuntide. His daily wage consisted of 11 Turonic solidi; he was permitted to eat at the abbot's table, the exact quantities and types of food allocated to him being carefully listed – this entitlement even extended to the times he ate away from the monastery. Each year at Whitsuntide he received 100 Turonic solidi to buy clothes. The agreement covered the period up to the completion of the church.

The two-way division of responsibilities for managing a large-scale building site is clear to see from this evidence. On the one hand there was a person in charge of technical construction, an experienced master builder who worked on the site itself, and on the other a master of works or head of buildings administration, responsible for financial management and organisation, the latter being elected by the monastery or town council for a period of one or two years. This pattern can be traced right through the Middle Ages as far back as Carolingian times.

The term 'architectus' which appears in the sources, pointed out by Nikolaus Pevsner in 1942 and Günther Binding in 1996, is used on the one hand for the founder of the church, the one whose contribution is to be understood in the symbolic sense of Paul's First Letter to the Corinthians: '... as a wise masterbuilder, I have laid the foundation'. On the other it is used to denote the mason who uses his skill actually to lay the foundations of the church. This conforms with the writings of Saint Thomas Aquinas in his *Summa theologiae,* begun after 1265 in Paris: 'Thus, in building, the craftsman (*artifex*) who designs the form of a building is called wise and architect (*architector*) as opposed to the subordinated craftsmen who hew wood or prepare stones, as described in 1 Corinthians 3.' This view reflects the metaphysics of Aristotle, whose teachings were very influential in the late 12th century in Paris and Chartres in particular. A 12th-century Latin translation of his work stated: 'The artificer (*artifex*) before those who have learned something through experience, the architect (*architector*) before the craftsman who works with his hands (*manu artifice*), thinking is more than the practical.' In a 12th-century collection of aphorisms this view is summarised as follows: 'The *artifex* as *architector* is wiser than the experienced *artifex* who works with his hands.'

In continuation of these thoughts Saint Thomas Aquinas wrote at Easter 1269 in Paris in his *Quaestiones de quodlibet:* 'It must be remembered that in any work of art (*artificium*) in a simple way, the one who gives orders with respect to that work of art and is called *architector,* is better than any labourer (*manualis*) who worked on the piece in accordance with orders given to him by another. For which reason in the construction of buildings the one who gives the orders with respect to the building, even though he may do nothing with his hands, earns a higher wage than the craftsmen (*manuales artifices*) who chop wood and hew stones.'

In this context, the Franciscan monk Nicholas de Biard complained in 1261: 'The master masons (*magistri cementariorum*), with measure and gloves in their hands, say to the others: cut me this. But they themselves do not work yet they receive a higher wage. This is how many prelates act these days.' In the *Distinctiones,* also ascribed to Nicholas de Biard, we read: 'Some work only with the word. Note: on these great buildings there is usually a main master (*magister principalis*) who works only through the word; seldom or never laying his own hand to the work, and yet he receives a higher wage than the others. Thus there are many in the church who have very comfortable posts and only God knows how much good they do. Their only work is of the tongue, and they say, this is how you should do it. Yet they themselves do none of it.'

This derision was rooted very much in the general religious and spiritual movement in the middle of the 13th century, in which the grumbling masses of the people made the high-living prelates and abbots a target of ridicule and mockery, even despising them and calling for Apostolic poverty. The money economy, division of labour in the cities, technical progress across a wide field and a universal lay culture in Europe had led to far-reaching structural change. In the course of this development in the 13th century the master craftsmen, the *artifices* or *magistri lapicidae,* also gained status and income in their role as technical managers of building works (*magistri operis*).

Gerhard, the master builder of Cologne cathedral, to whom is generally attributed the planning and construction of the first stage of rebuilding the new section from 1248 onwards, was given by the Cologne cathedral chapter in 1257, in recognition of his services to the cathedral church, the hereditary leasehold on a particularly large piece of land on which he had built, from his own means, a large stone house. In an undated document detailing the conditions of his will we learn that this house in Marzellenstrasse was so large that it could be divided into four apartments. From the documentation about his estate it also becomes clear that Master Gerhard owned three other houses in Marzellenstrasse. House ownership by master craftsmen described as *magistri* is proven by a number of other sources from the 13th century. The master builder of Paris cathedral, Pierre de Montreuil, is named in connection with acquiring property – in 1247 in Saint-Denis and in 1265 in Paris. In addition he owned a piece of land and a quarry in Conflans near Charenton, a property in Cachan, and in 1265 he sold a property in Vauvert to the monastery in Chartreux. House ownership is evidence of high social status for the master builder.

In parallel with this rise in personal status we see at the end of the second half of the 13th century more and more gravestones for master builders, such as that of Hugues Libergier of Reims († 1263), which was probably not made until the end of the 13th century. The names of master builders were now being recorded for posterity in labyrinth patterns inlaid into church floors, in reference to the legendary architect Daedalus, who built the Labyrinth of Knossos on Crete: names such as Robert de Luzarches, Thomas Cormont and his son Regnault in 1288 in the cathedral of Amiens; or, inscribed in the cathedral of Reims after 1290, the names of those master builders involved from 1211 onwards – Jean d'Orbais, Jean le Loup, Gaucher de Reims and Bernard de Soissons. In memory of his predecessor, Jean de Chelles, who died in 1258, Pierre de Montreuil even had the following inscription, 10 m long and 8 cm high, carved in stone in the base of the south transept: 'In February 1257 this was begun ... by the master stonemason Johann [who was then still living].'

Pages 66 and 67
Small but beautiful
The abbot's chapel of the Cistercian monastery of Chaalis near
Fontaine on the Oise dates from
the middle of the 13th century
(restored). Triple-panelled tracery
windows are inserted between the
vaulting shafts.

Pages 68 and 69
Cistercian abbey of Chaalis near Fontaine on the Oise
King Louis VI founded this monastery for monks from Pontigny after the murder of his brother Charles the Good. The church was used as a burial chapel for the bishops of Senlis. Now mostly in ruins, it was built 1202–1219. On the left is the much restored abbot's chapel dating from the mid-13th century.

The higher status of master of works is unmistakable in the illustration of c. 1250 depicting the life of King Offa by Matthew Paris, who was a monk in St Albans. Shown in this illustration are three persons entering the building site: first King Offa with sceptre, and behind him, designated by his leather cap, spirit level and pair of compasses, the master builder, and the well-dressed buildings administrator. On the building site are masons, stonemasons, carpenters, labourers and winch boys, each working with the tools of his trade.

Division of Labour on a Medieval Building Site

On the building sites of Gothic cathedrals a number of different groups of crafts-men (*artifices, operarii*) and helpers (*garciones, famuli, servi, knechte*) were employed, as well as a stoking boy, several mortar-makers (*morteliers*), winch boys and earth-workers (*fodiatores*). Specialist workers included masons (*caementarii, lathomi, muratores,* since 1271 *murer*), stonemasons and sculptors (*lapicidae, sculptores, cae-sores lapidum*), carpenters (*carpentarii*), smiths (*fabri*), at times also roofers (*tegula-tores*), ropemakers and glaziers, and, in the stone quarry, stonebreakers (*fractores lapidum, incisores in lapidicina, quarriatores*). On the list of the highest wages, put together after the city fire of London in 1212, the building trades recorded were: carpenter, mason, roofer, stonemason/sculptor, whitewasher, loam plasterer, plasterer and glazier. The list of all the available trades in Paris, put together in 1268 on the orders of King Louis IX, mentioned the following among to the building trades: masons (*macons*), stonemasons (*tailleurs de pierre*), plasterers (*plastieres*), mortar-makers (*morteliers*), carpenters (*charpentiers*) and joiners (*huissiers*).

At Westminster Abbey, which was rebuilt by King Henry III, some 435 persons were employed between the middle of June and 20 July 1253. They included 130 stonemasons and 220 labourers, plus marble-workers, polishers, masons, carpen-ters, smiths, lead-pourers and glaziers. During harvest time in September 1253 the

number went down to about 200, most of those who left being labourers. After the harvest, by 9 November, up to 160 labourers were again engaged. Following that there were only the specialist craftsmen, now a smaller group, but still amounting to 100 men.

Working on the Vale Royal Abbey (1278–1280) near Northwich were on average 135 craftsmen and labourers, with as many as 231 in June 1278. In that year there were at times 64 stonemasons working at the same time on the site, with 39 in 1279 and 51 in 1280; the average period of engagement was five to ten months. Of the 30 stonemasons employed in 1280, 11 spent longer than two years (29–36 months) at the site, four spent 12 months. In Exeter in 1299/1300 on average 30 persons were present on the site, including 15 stonemasons and nine labourers. The names recorded as having worked on the Vale Royal church show that all the 486 carters, earthworkers and stonemasons came from that area, but only about half of the 71 carpenters and smiths and only 5 to 10 % of the 131 stonemasons. Again and again the sources describe the acquisition of stonemasons as a particular concern.

Simple Tools for Complicated Building Work

The stonemasons, carpenters and smiths worked out in the open air, either on the building site or in an area next to it. However, light shelters would have given some protection against the rain. It was not until the 13th century that wooden huts gradually came into use to enable stonemasons to continue their work in the winter. The tools that became common on these sites throughout the Middle Ages were modest in both number and quality, and indeed differed little from those used from ancient times right through to the 19th century. Masons had trowels, hammers, plumb lines, spirit levels and blades to mix the mortar, while stonemasons used pointed and flat-bladed chisels, flatteners, mallets, angles, straight-edges and compasses. Carpenters used axes, hatchets, saws, chisels, mallets, straight-edges and coloured string.

In the 12th century, stones or shaped pieces had been part-finished in the quarries, in order to facilitate transport. But it was not until the 13th century that standardisation had been introduced, that is, prefabrication or series production. While in the cathedrals in Laon and Bourges traditional individual production of pieces can be found, there is evidence of standardisation in the choirs of the cathedrals of Soissons and Chartres. Series production was first seen in the nave of the cathedral of Amiens, where 28 compound piers were constructed identically using two basic block types. By comparison, in Reims, for the same kind of pillar, eight different types were chosen, which even at the time was considered to be quite unusual, as Villard de Honnecourt recorded precise joint drawings in his pattern book in 1220/1230.

This new technique, which first appeared around 1220, enabled stonemasons to be employed in greater numbers in winter, too (with time in summer being used to lay the stones), thus shortening the total construction time and making better use of specialist craftsmen. At the same time it also promoted a more formal approach to the design: in other words, scale drawings became necessary, along with templates and construction plans. The first step, seen from around 1200, was to prepare scratched drawings of individual building components such as tracery windows to a scale of 1:1, then whole sections of the building were drawn, such as the palimpsest of the west façade of Reims around 1240/1250. When Villard de Honnecourt was in Reims in around 1220/1230, however, he did not come across such plans there.

A stonemason at work
A stonemason uses a flattener and hammer to work on a capital. (Redrawn from the *Bible Moralisée*, second quarter of the 13th century, Vienna, Österreichische Nationalbibliothek, Cod. 2554, fol. 50ᵛ)

Transporting Building Materials

Building materials were transported to the site on water wherever possible, either on barges or rafts; transport over land was on two- or four-wheeled ox carts, and in the case of particularly heavy loads on rollers or sleds. On the site itself smaller weights were carried in wheelbarrows, on wooden pallets moved by two men, in a wood carrier across the shoulder, in baskets or on a 'oisseau', two crossed poles carried over the shoulders. Sloping runners were used to transport material up to the higher levels, or alternatively the material, such as stones or mortar, was placed in a basket or bucket or on pallets, to be hauled up by rope over a crossbeam or boom. Larger stones were tied with rope using, until the middle of the 13th century, a 'rack', which was a three-part iron suspension attachment hooked in a swallow-tail notch in the surface of the stone. From the beginning of the 13th century a kind of stone grab had become common, whereby prongs were inserted into two small, square or round holes worked into the front and back of the block to lever it up to the required level.

Descriptions from the 12th and early 13th centuries provide evidence that building techniques were gradually catching up with those used in Late antiquity and in the East during the Byzantine period. Around 1100 a type of crane appeared to move loads. It had two uprights, joined by a crossbeam around which was wound a length of rope. Also in use was a standing crane with a T-shaped boom on top, the rope being at the end of this boom. Both basic types were to be found from the end of the 13th century.

Building material was generally lifted aloft by winch boys. The earliest form of a medieval winch, dating from the 13th century, is a windlass with a horizontal shaft affixed to two wooden posts or a trestle-like construction; the windlass was operated using hand spokes or winders. It seems that the crane with running wheel, a device already known in antiquity, was not used in France for Gothic buildings until the middle of the 13th century. By the 14th century, however, this piece of equipment had become quite common across Europe. The running wheel was driven by the body weight of one or more winch boys running inside the drum, with the longer axis of the drum serving as the winch itself. With this device it was possible to move heavier stone blocks up to any desired height. Already by around 1180 in Paris and in Laon the stone blocks found in the upper reaches of the cathedral are clearly bigger, and in the cathedral of Soissons, even before 1212, workpieces found in vaults and window reveals were made from monolithic slabs weighing several tons.

Gervase of Canterbury particularly admired the ingenuity of the winches constructed by the French master builder William of Sens for loading and offloading the stones brought to the city by sea from northern France in 1175 for use in the construction of the cathedral. In 1220/1230 Villard de Honnecourt, in his pattern book, also studied the construction of various machines, but he gave no account of a crane with running wheel.

For setting and laying the stones working platforms on trestle, boom or standing scaffold arrangements became necessary. Material was hauled up on sloping runners, ladders being used only for workers' access to the higher level platforms. The scaffolding was put together by the carpenters, who also built and set up the support frames and guiding arches for the stone arches and vaults. They also made the roof frame which could itself serve as a working platform for constructing the roof vault.

Progress of Construction

With this relatively simple, traditional equipment and in a short space of time, these splendid cathedrals and monastery churches, much marvelled at, were built – given an influential patron, sufficient building materials and funding, as well as the requisite number of specialist craftsmen.

Hauling stones and mortar
A hoist is used to haul up mortar in a wooden barrel and a stone block held by a grab. Below, a labourer is mixing mortar with a spade. (Redrawn from the Manuscript from the world chronicle of Jansen Enikel, fol. 21, c. 1380, Regensburg, Fürstlich Thurn- und Taxissche Hofbibliothek)

The Building Plan – Drawn Only in the Head of the Master Builder

Generally, and contrary to popular belief, buildings constructed up to the middle of the 13th century were carried out largely without the aid of any construction drawings. The basis for the whole project was at first just the idea of the type of building and the dimensions, as envisaged in the mind (*in mente conceptum*) of the master builder. The architectural design did not take on its final form until the empirical stage of actually working with the materials during construction of the building. The spatial design and proportions were laid down to an established convention, set out in the form of brief instructions, and contained, for example, in the contracts with master craftsmen for their contribution to the building. Only when work was under way were individual components etched out as scratched drawings, to a scale of 1:1, as already described.

From the second quarter of the 13th century projections started to be etched with great care, 2–3 mm deep, in stone or plastered wall surfaces or on terraced roofs. We know of 16 examples from France, 13 from England, nine from Germany and one from Dalmatia. The earliest floor etching preserved from this time and also reliably dated is in Soissons and comes from the middle of the 13th century. It shows a blind arcade and tracery window. The projections in Bourges (tracery window), Clermont-Ferrand, Limoges, Narbonne and Cambridge were created around 1300. Such projections, on a scale of 1:1, were used for measuring out templates and checking the dimensions of stones before building with them.

The oldest preserved scale projections (elevations) on parchment are the two Reims palimpsests with the triple-portalled façade of a church. These were done in around 1250/1260 by the same hand that drew copies of examples from the period around 1230/1250. In 1220/1230 in Reims Villard de Honnecourt had no such projections as a model for the drawings in his pattern book, but he had developed ground plans which included details of wall thicknesses. In around 1260/1270 the oldest Strasbourg Projections – A and A' – were created for a partial elevation of the west façade of the minster; Projection B was drawn around 1275 and D in around 1277/1280 (perhaps by Erwin of Steinbach). Projections from other building sites also come from the last quarter of the 13th century, like the oldest preserved ground plan (Viennese Projection A) for the southwest tower of Cologne cathedral, around 1280, and Cologne Projection F for the west façade, prepared around 1300.

The written sources also confirm this period as the time in which small-scale plan drawings started to emerge. Robert Grosseteste, who was educated in Paris, knew of no such plans, as deduced from his letter to Adam Rufus in 1228/1232. Saint Thomas Aquinas, too, made the assumption in his *Summa theologiae*, begun in Paris in 1265, that 'the master of building works [*artifex*] strives to give the building the form which he has conceived in his head'. Abbot Menko of Wittewierum near Groningen in Holland wrote in 1248: 'Because it is difficult to continue building if you do not know the intention of the first founder, particularly as that excellent master of building works [*artifex*] had first deposited the design of his work in his head, ... therefore we describe at this point the initial conception of the work, so that when it pleases our successors to continue building, they have therein the design [*materia*] of that which is to be continued.' In his *Speculum maius,* in around 1250, Vincent of Beauvais, teacher and librarian at the court of Louis IX, mentioned an *ichnographia,* which, in the tradition of Vitruvius, is a small-scale ground plan of a building. This mention came at the same time as the first Reims projections and the pattern book of Villard de Honnecourt.

On this basis it is hard to imagine that complicated proportional figures were used for measuring ground plans and elevations. Instead the key information was contained in simple triangular constructions (such as were common in measuring ground plans since Antiquity) and whole numbers of foot measures. Such a system was still being used in 1391–1400, as seen in a discussion among master builders invited to assess the correct dimensions for the construction of the nave of the cathedral in Milan, which 'was done according to the geometric logic of the triangle'.

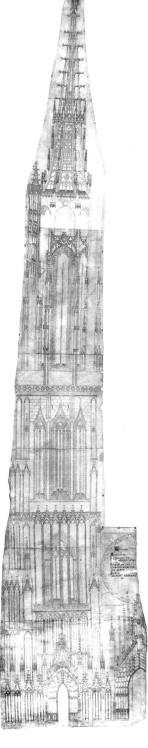

Northwest tower of Strasbourg minster
Design sketch or working drawing from the late 13th century. (Bern, Suisse; Bernisches Historisches Museum)

Design sketch for stonemasons
Preserved on the roof terrace above the long south choir of the cathedral of Clermont-Ferrand is an etched drawing which is an actual-size representation of the openwork gablet of the south transept portal. The stonemasons could use the drawing to check whether the workpieces hewn by them were the right size to fit into the overall construction.

A very precise picture of the preparations for building a large Gothic church emerges from the detailed accounts for the first three years of construction work on the Vale Royal Abbey (1278–1280) in England. In the first year the carpenters erected two forges, one in the quarry and one on the building site; here a smith and an assistant mended tools on a wood-fired hearth, while a second assistant operated the bellows, and a third collected and delivered hammers, drills and stone-working tools at the site. Sleeping quarters for the stonemasons and other craftsmen were erected and whitewashed, as well as a stone house for the master builder. In June 1279 a bill was paid for 1 400 boards for the workshops of the stonemasons, and a further 2 000 boards were acquired in April 1280. In total in the three years 12 300 wooden boards were sawn and 67 000 iron nails bought for the construction of work sheds and housing.

At the same time as the carpenters started their work six gangs of eight workers each began to extract stone from the nearby quarry. In March 1277 labourers were busy 'levelling the floor on which the ground plan of the monastery was to be marked'. In April of the following year 200 men shovelled 'banks and ditches for a pond from which water could be channelled to the building site for making mortar'. In July 1278 44 labourers were engaged in 'digging out and laying the foundations for the church, mixing mortar and bringing it over, digging out sand and pushing wheelbarrows'. In January 1280 the same work was being done by 18 labourers.

Gervase was a contemporary witness of the progress of construction work on Canterbury cathedral in the years 1175–1179, when William of Sens was master of building works (*artifex*). In 1185 Gervase wrote: 'And now he addressed himself to procuring stone from overseas [Continent]. He constructed ingenious machines for loading and unloading ships and for drawing cement and stones. He delivered moulds for shaping the stones to the sculptors who were assembled, and diligently prepared other things of the same kind. The choir thus condemned to destruction was pulled down, and nothing else was done in this year [September 1174–September 1175]. ...

In the following year, that is, after the feast of Saint Bertin [5 September 1175], before the winter, he erected four pillars, that is, two on each side, and after winter two more were placed, so that on each side were three in order, upon which and upon the exterior wall of the aisles he framed seemly arches and a vault, that is three *claves* [keystones or bosses] on each side. I put *clavis* for the whole vault because the *clavis* placed in the middle locks up and binds together the parts which converge to it from every side. ... In the third year [September 1176–September 1177] he added two more pillars on each side, and decorated the two outer ones all around with marble columns, and because this is the point at which the choir and the arms of the transept are to come together, he fashioned these as the main pillars. And after the finishing stones were placed on these and the vaults constructed, he spanned the lower triforium with many marble columns between the larger tower and the aforementioned pillars, that is to the transept. Above this triforium he placed another triforium made out of a different material and the upper windows, then added three finishing stones in the great vault, from the tower to the transept. ...

In the summer of 1178 he erected ten pillars starting at the transept, five on each side. Decorating the first two with marble pillars, he formed them into main pillars opposite the other two. Over these ten he placed the arches and vault. And having, in the next place, completed on both sides the triforia and upper windows, he prepared the scaffolding for the grand vaulted ceiling at the beginning of the fifth year [September 1178]. [It was then that the master and the scaffolding fell to the ground] ... Thus was created the vaulted ceiling between the four main pillars, in whose finishing stone it can be said the choir and the arms of the transept seem to come together. Also, before the winter two [more] vaults were constructed on both sides, but the increasingly heavy rainfall did not permit more to be done. ...

Gravestone of the master builder of Reims
The gravestone of Hugues Libergier, master builder of the Benedictine abbey of Saint-Nicaise in Reims († 1263), was probably carved at the end of the 13th century. Today it can be seen in the cathedral of Reims. The master is depicted wearing a shirt, coat and cap; he holds before him a model of the church and in his left hand a measuring stick. Next to his feet are a straight-edge and compasses, with which he draws the plans.

A Gothic building site
Representation of a French building site in the middle of the 13th century as an illustration of the Tower of Babel in the Old Testament. Labourers carry stones on a platform and mortar in a wooden trough over their shoulders up a ladder-like walkway leading up to the masons who lay the blocks with a trowel and hammer. Using a hoist and wheel pulley, seen here for the first time on a medieval illustration, stones are hauled up. At the bottom right two stonemasons are busy measuring up a block with their straight-edge and dressing it with hammer and flattener. (New York, Pierpont Morgan Library, Ms. fr. 638, fol. 3)

In the summer of the fifth year [1179] both transepts, the southernmost and the northernmost, were completed along with the vault above the main altar which could not be built the previous year, although everything had been prepared, because of the rain. He also made the foundations in the eastern part of the church extension, because the Chapel to Saint Thomas was to be rebuilt there. ... Having, therefore, formed a most substantial foundation for the exterior wall with stone and cement, he erected the wall of the crypt as high as the bases of the windows. This completed the fifth year of construction [September 1179].'

Some buildings were erected in an amazingly short period of time. We know for example that, in the case of the abbey church of Saint-Denis, the westwork was finished between 1130/1135 and 1140 and the choir was constructed in just three years and eleven months, from 1141 to the end of 1144. The basic shell for the Sainte-Chapelle in Paris, the palace chapel of the French king, was built between 1241 and 1245 and the choir of Canterbury between 1175 and 1183, when work was halted for lack of money. The Premonstratensian monastery church of Saint-Yved in Braine was completed in about nine years (c. 1204), and construction work on the decagon of St Gereon in Cologne took just eight years (1219–1227).

What Price a Cathedral? And Who Pays?

As a rule sufficient funds were available for buildings when the patron was the king. Monasteries, too, were capable of making substantial monies available by collecting or concentrating their income. It was a different case with bishop and collegiate churches. Generally the bishops, canons and prebendaries gave only small sums from their private purses. The bulk of the money had to come instead from church income, donations and non-assigned prebends and benefices (payments to canons). These items, however, were annual payments and for various reasons the flow of money to the *fabrica,* the financial administrators of the site, and to the coffers of the church building fund could abate, come to a complete standstill or be interrupted, as happened in 1233 in Reims because of a dispute between the town authorities and the bishop. Sometimes it became necessary to supplement the regular income by selling forests or land. Larger donations from the nobility or the king were usually only for interior fixtures and fittings, in particular stained-glass windows. As, in most cases, the new building had been prompted by the destruction of the old one by fire, emotions were at first high and people were correspondingly free with their donations. The miraculous rescue of the robe of the Virgin from Chartres was interpreted by them as a sign from God. As building work progressed, however, enthusiasm tended to wane.

The individual church's miracle-working reliquaries were even despatched 'on tour' to bring in additional revenue. In his autobiography, Guibert, abbot of Nogent from 1104 († 1124), mentioned clerics who travelled from place to place in northern France and Flanders, taking with them reliquaries from Laon and collecting donations. He related how they were tricked by tradesmen and on the crossing to England robbed by pirates. For seven months they then travelled through towns in the south of England, returning finally to Laon laden with rich donations. In this way additional sums were added to the funds already available for the building work.

In the end, however, all attempts to establish how much a particular building project cost are doomed to failure, not because the sources tell us too little about the level of donations or expenditure, but because they never give information about the total funding needed for a recognisable phase of building. Nor do they indicate the extent to which payment in kind, such as the provision of materials or food, transport and socage, were included, all of which would have been significant factors in the cost of building work. In 1196/1197 Richard the Lionheart gave £55 000 sterling (around 220 000 Turonic solidi) from the royal coffers for the building of Château-Gaillard, and to this were added the services of the people living nearby. When, for example, we learn that £40 000 in Turonic solidi were used for building the Sainte-Chapelle in Paris, while a medium-sized house in the city cost £150, then we have to remember that for the construction of this relatively small chapel, almost exclusively highly specialised craftsmen would have been needed – stonemasons, glaziers, painters and the like. And that the mid-13th century was already a time in which craftsmen were increasingly paid in money and less with goods and benefits.

Page 77
Building work
In this representation of forced labour by Jews under the Babylonians (Paris, 13th century) the master builder, with measuring stick, kneels before his king; stonemasons dress a piece of stone using flatteners and hammers, and check the edges using an angle guide. A labourer carries stones in a hod up a wooden ladder. A mason stands on a scaffold and lays stones with mortar taken from wooden containers. (New York, Pierpont Morgan Library, Ms. fr. 638, fol. 7)

A Medieval Pattern Book – The Drawings of Villard de Honnecourt

'Vilars dehonecort' is how the author of the pattern book, consisting of 33 parchment sheets (16 x 24 cm), now held in the National Library in Paris (ms. fr. 19093), signed himself. Villard, from Honnecourt in Picardy, was probably a master of works (*artifex*), and he drew the sketches in around 1220/1230 on his journeys to Cambrai, Meaux, Vaucelles, Reims, Laon, Chartres, Lausanne and Hungary. He later collected them together in a *livre*, organised thematically and supplemented with explanatory annotations, partly written by himself, and partly by two other masters over the course of the 13th century.

Thirteen of the sheets went missing that same century. Two-thirds of the 325 drawings still in existence are representations of people (163 drawings) and animals (62), the remainder being drawings of liturgical equipment and machinery, elevations and ground plans of churches and four pages of geometry for building. The brown pen drawings were sketched out first in pencil and those of buildings also in blind grooves on parchment. In the drawings which can still be compared to the original structures in Reims, Laon, Chartres and Lausanne, it is evident that Villard altered the building forms slightly according to his own understanding of construction geometry, and in part summarised what was there.

His figural drawings belong in diverse iconographic areas of sculpture, book illumination and glass painting: Christian figures, allegories, personifications of the ecclesia, scenes from courts of law and tournaments, dice players and fights with lions as well as nudes, probably drawn from ancient Greek or Roman sculptures. The many animal representations with geometric figures as an aid to drawing are in the tradition of bestiaries, or mythical zoological representations of the appearance and behaviour of animals, recorded in Alexandria and much copied and supplemented in the 12th century in particular. In many ways Villard's sketches are sources for deeper insight into the planning techniques used at the time. They are particularly informative in the case of the cathedral of Reims, which was extremely influential in the development of the High Gothic, in formal terms because of its articulating piers, its tracery and its sculptural programme, in terms of planning and technology (in 1211/1233) because of the inclusion of building projections and the palimpsests of Reims in the middle of the 13th century.

Pages 78 and 79

A master builder's pattern book
The Parisian pattern book written by Villard de Honnecourt in 1220/1230 contains elevations of the Lady chapel of Reims cathedral – Sheet 30 shows an exterior elevation (*page 78, top*) and Sheet 31 shows an interior elevation (*page 79, top left*). This chapel was built 1211–1220 and has one of the oldest tracery windows in existence. Sheet 10 is a representation of an elevation, in foreshortened perspective, of one of the west towers of the cathedral of Laon (*page 79, top right*): 'Nowhere have I ever seen such a tower as at Laon.' On Sheet 31ᵛ are interior and exterior elevations of a bay of the nave in Reims cathedral, shown in parallel to clarify the links between inside and outside (*page 78, bottom*); the flying buttresses (*page 79, top centre*) and the vault were still to be constructed. Sheet 32 presents details of the pillars and profiles (*page 79, bottom left*). The upper of the two ground plans on Sheet 15 was designed by Villard and Peter of Corbie 'in joint collaboration with each other'; the lower plan shows Saint-Faron in Meaux (*page 79, centre bottom*). On Sheet 29 Villard drew a design for the end of a choir stall (*page 79, bottom right*).

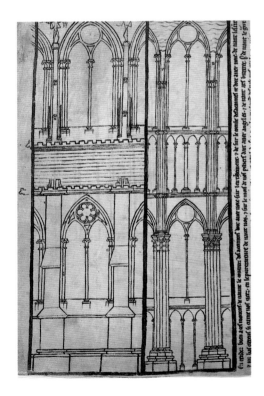

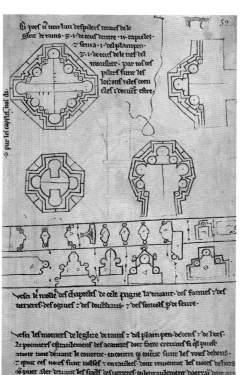

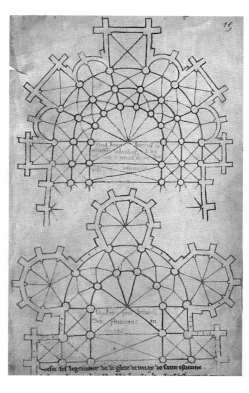

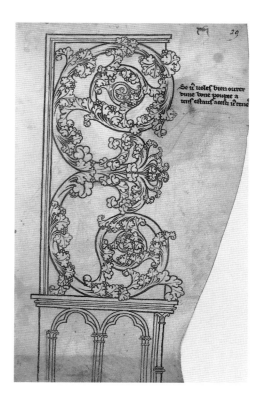

AN INTERPLAY OF FORCES

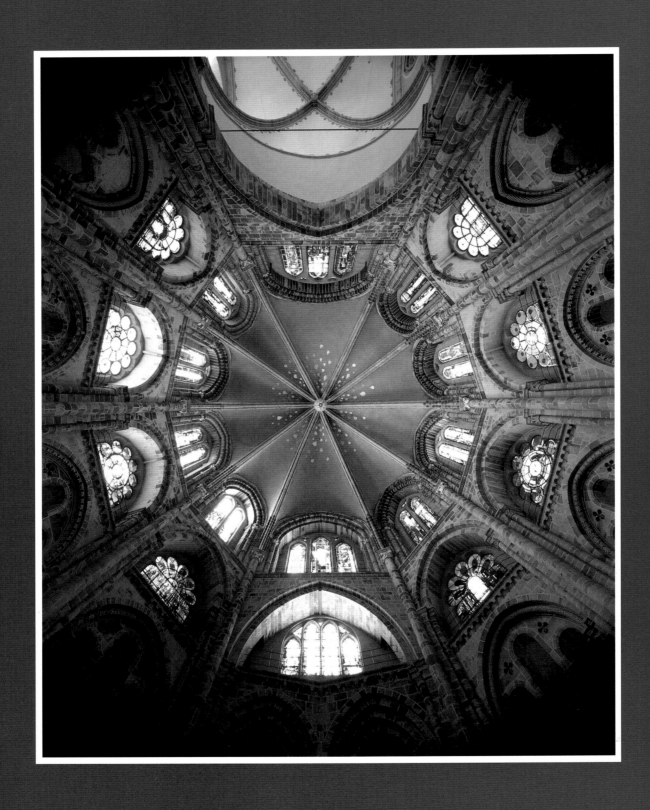

Bold Constructions for Spatial Effect

The decagon of St Gereon, Cologne
This masterpiece by a Rhenish builder who was familiar with cathedral building projects in France was designed as an oval structure in the Roman conch style (1219–1227). Thick, round vaulting shafts rise from the floor into the heights to carry ten ribs which come together in a central, leather-covered wooden boss; the sections of the vault stretch between the ribs like sails.

The Illusion of Floating

The basic form of the Gothic cathedral is the same as that commonly used for Christian churches since Late Antiquity – a basilica divided into three aisles (rarely five), with the central section raised above the sides. Light enters through windows in the upper part, the clerestory. From the turn of the millennium in central France, particularly in the Auvergne, galleries were placed above the vaults of the side aisles, opening up as arcades to the central aisle. In the second half of the 11th century such galleries started to emerge in Normandy and in England. In around the middle of the 12th century the structural significance of the gallery vaults as a component in the distribution of vault thrust from the central aisle came to be recognised. The master builders in the heartland of Gothic architecture – in the Île-de-France, the Champagne district and Picardy – started to use galleries over the side aisles and in the choir as well as in the triple-aisled transept as a key element in construction. Then, between 1150 and 1260, the first vaulted central aisles in the central and lower Rhine districts began to appear – at Speyer (1100–1120) and Worms (1130–1181).

This triple tier of arcade, gallery and clerestory was extended in the middle of the 12th century by adding a triforium between the gallery and the window zone (probably inspired by Anglo-Norman models). The resulting four-tier arrangement of the wall became characteristic of the Early Gothic, good examples being the cathedrals of Senlis, Noyon, Laon, Paris from 1163 and Notre-Dame-en-Vaux in Châlons-sur-Marne (Châlons-en-Champagne) around 1170. Here the ribs of the vault spring from bundles of vaulting shafts which, in Châlons-sur-Marne, Laon, Paris and Saint-Remi in Reims, lead only as far as the imposts of the round masonry columns with capitals; this gives the impression that the entire upper structure is, as it were, detached from the floor.

After 1194, with the construction of Chartres cathedral, the gallery was abandoned, leaving the classic Gothic triple-tiered wall consisting of arcade, triforium and window zone, as subsequently used in Reims and Amiens. Also in Chartres the sexpartite rib vault linking two bays was replaced by the quadripartite rib vault over each transverse oblong bay. The face wall framed by one rib is largely broken up by two closely set lancet windows under a large circle with eight-lobed tracery. Together with the row triforium and the vaulting shafts in front of the alternately round and octagonal columns, there arises an evenly designed sequence of pierced wall areas between the vaulting shafts. It is the first stage towards structured, geometric and linear 'latticing', which was completed with the introduction of the tracery window in Reims (1211–1233); in other words, this marked the breaking up of the wall plane, an effect that was finally made possible through the extensive system of buttresses and flying buttresses used in Chartres. The special nature of this articulation, perfected in Reims, was carefully recorded in drawings by Villard de Honnecourt around 1220/1230 on his visit to the building site there. By drawing the interior and exterior elevations of a bay next to one another he clarified their alignment.

Hans Jantzen described this articulation of the walls exemplified in Reims as a 'diaphanous structure' and 'a relief grid backed by a spatial structure of differing depth and optical character depending on the position of the various levels. ... The wall as a border for the entire interior of the main part of the nave can only be understood in terms of the overall depth of space, and it is through this that it achieves its effect. The spatial depth itself appears as an optical zone behind the wall, as it were.'

This idea of the main part of the nave being surrounded by a spatial shell is a fundamental observation, which finds its explanation in the liturgical practice of the cathedral. The central part of the choir, that is, the area with the altar and choir stalls, spatially enclosed and given a basilical air by the ambulatory with radiating chapels, continues in the equal-height crossing of the central nave, four bays of which belong to the choir, as we know from Reims. The middle of the church, in other words the west-east axis, with main altar, lay altar and processional routes, is the core area for liturgical practice, and its ceremonial effect is heightened all along this axis, from the west portal right down the main part of the nave. The side aisles, like the side aisles in the transept, and the ambulatory of the choir are peripheral liturgical zones off the main area of nave and choir. The pierced end wall of the choir and the dominant rose windows at the ends of the transept and in the west wall play a key role in marking out the main axis – these light sources, with their figural depictions in the stained glass, are, in both a spatial and a religious sense, determining factors in the limits of this core area.

In rebuilding work at Saint-Denis after 1231 and in the choir at Troyes before 1241, an attempt was made to heighten even more the effect of the stained-glass

Pages 84 and 85
Saint-Quiriace, Provins / Seine-et-Marne
The collegiate church of the counts of Champagne was begun shortly after 1157, and the choir was probably completed by 1166. Work continued on the transept and the nave until 1238. The crossing tower is Baroque. In its triple-storey articulation (arcades, triforium, windows) and architectural details, the choir reveals the influence of Sens cathedral, in the diocese of which Provins lies. The slim, ringed vaulting shafts start on the capitals of the round pillars and carry the stilted ribbed arches.

windows as a light source, by leading the window bars down via the now illuminated triforium to create a unified light zone over the arcades. This is matched in the transept walls by the merging of the rose window with the row of windows below into a façade completely broken down into tracery. Examples of this are the north transept of the cathedral of Paris, designed by Jean de Chelles around 1245–1258, the south transept of that same cathedral designed by the master builder Pierre de Montreuil after 1258, and Châlons-sur-Marne from 1256. In the same period the bays in the tympanum of the west portal of the cathedral of Reims were illuminated with tracery. Finally this solution led to the two-tier elevation of arcades and window zones, such as initially, around 1230, in Lorraine, and in the royal collegiate and parish church of Notre-Dame-de-l'Assomption in Villeneuve-sur-Yonne in the diocese of Sens around 1240. It became predominant, too, in Germany, after 1235 in Marburg and Trier, while France continued with the three-tier wall elevation even in the 14th century.

Also noticeable is a steady increase in the internal height, with Noyon and Senlis at 22 m, Sens and Laon at 24.5 m, Paris at 33 m, Chartres at 34.65 m, Bourges at 37.15 m, Reims at 38 m, Amiens at 42.3 m, Cologne at 43.35 m, and Beauvais at 48.2 m. When in 1284, 12 years after its completion, part of the choir of Beauvais cathedral collapsed, it became clear that the structural limits to the breadth of the arcades and the height of the vault apex had been overstepped. In its reconstruction, completed in 1324, the arcade spacing was halved and sexpartite rib vaults were used.

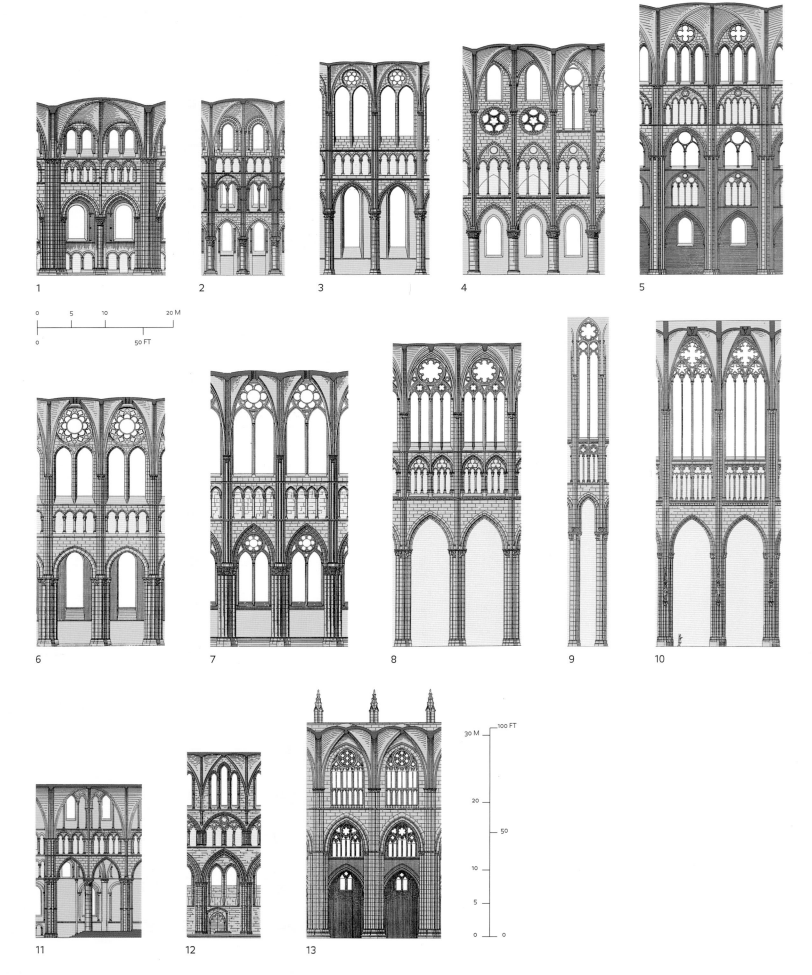

1

2

3

4

5

6

7

8

9

10

11

12

13

Quadripartite wall elevation
The south conch of the cathedral
of Soissons was begun in 1176.
The quadripartite wall elevation
consists of arcades, gallery, row
triforium and clerestory with
windows.

Compound Piers, Pillars and Columns

The formal differences between pillar, column, pilaster and vaulting shaft have to be taken very seriously in investigating the form of Gothic supports, if one is to understand the various stages in development. A close analysis shows that the master builders of the Middle Ages had a very refined sense of form. This is backed up by Gervase of Canterbury who, in 1185, when describing the cathedral of Canterbury, wrote of 'columns which are commonly called pillars' (*Columpnae, quae vulgo pilarii dicuntur*). He goes on to differentiate: after removal of the old choir 'he erected four pillars [*pilarios*] before the winter [1175]. ... In the third year [1177] he added two pillars [*pilarios*] on each side; the outer ones he intermingled with many marble columns [*columpnis*], and there, at the point where choir and transept arms come together, he formed them into main pillars [*principales pilarios*].'

In another place he remarked that the capitals of the 28 pillars in the circle of the choir were extremely finely sculpted. The five pillars still preserved on each side of the choir are alternately round and octagonal, and built up from dressed stone blocks. These straight pillars (they do not taper) carry suitably foliated capitals and low, profiled imposts. Black Purbeck marble columns whose smaller, lower capitals and upper shafts overlap the capitals of the round pillars encircle the two eastern crossing piers. The impost is laid uniformly across piers and columns. Gervase clearly used the word 'column' to refer to those with slim, monolithic shafts, while a pillar is for him a thick masonry support, be it round, octagonal or with a capital.

Early Gothic cathedral of Laon
View of the north wall of the nave (1180–1190) with arcades, galleries and triforium, richly articulated with bundles of three and five vaulting shafts with shaft rings. The sexpartite vault dictates the column alternation.

Early Gothic cathedral of Lincoln
Lincoln cathedral was built
1192–1230. Octagonal pillars with
vaulting shafts of Purbeck marble
(as in Canterbury) support triple
vaulting ribs. Above the moulding
between the storeys, the galleries
open with double or triple arches
on columns and perforated arched
openings below graduated archivolts. The windows in the clerestory are behind a wall passage
with graduated arches.

Gervase's understanding of these terms corresponds to our modern terminology. A pillar, as distinct from a section of wall, has to have an impost, and can be separated from the ground by a base or a pedestal; the main shaft of a pillar is made up
of masonry blocks which may be rectangular, octagonal, circular or cruciform. A pillar does not taper towards the top. By contrast a column always has a base, a shaft
and a capital and generally also an impost. As a rule the (sometimes decorated) shaft
is monolithic, but it may also be made of column drums, and it may be circular,
octagonal or spiral in shape; its cross-section often tapers towards the neck (start
of the capital). Pillars and columns may take the form of projections from a wall
(called engaged pillars or columns) and be combined with each other. If the shaft of
an engaged column has a square cross-section or if the engaged pillar has a capital,
then this is termed a pilaster – still termed a *columna quadrangular* by Leon Battista
Alberti in 1485. If the shaft of an engaged column is exaggeratedly long and does
not taper, we refer to this component, which generally takes a rib vault, as a vaulting shaft. The vaulting shaft in the Early and High Gothic usually has a base and a
capital.

Choir ambulatory of Chartres
cathedral
The choir ambulatory was built following a fire in 1194. A characteristic feature is the alternation
between round and octagonal pillars with capitals and partly projecting vaulting shafts, a precursor
of the compound pier.

The change in the understanding of the column and the pillar is particularly
clear in the choir of Saint-Denis, built by Abbot Suger in 1140–1144; his *columnae*
correspond in all respects to the traditional development: they have a base, a capital and an impost, but their monolithic shafts do not taper towards the top.
Depending on their location the shafts are either thick, thin, compact or slim in profile, as after 1176 in the south transept of the cathedral of Soissons, in around 1200
in the choir of the collegiate church of Notre-Dame-en-Vaux in Châlons-sur-Marne
and in Saint-Remi in Reims (1170/1180). The plinth and the base pedestal are bevelled at the corners. The inner choir columns were not replaced by masonry ones
until the renovation of the choir of Saint-Denis after 1231, when, on the side facing
the choir, a vaulting shaft was added for which an impost then had to be made. This
is similar to forms in the choir (c. 1200–1212) and in the nave (until c. 1230) of the
cathedral of Soissons, in the cathedral of Beauvais (1227–1245), in the choir of the
cathedral of Clermont-Ferrand (1248–1280) and in the cathedral of Meaux (after
1253).

**Nave and choir of the cathedral
of Reims**
Round pillars with four projecting vaulting shafts and unified
capitals. On the columns on the
west side they merge to form a
ring of capitals, thus creating
the classic Gothic compound or
membered pier. The bays on the
east of the nave were built around
1220–1233, those on the west
around 1250.

The combination of a non-tapering masonry column, made up of column drums
and having slim projecting columns, was used around 1177–1196 by the second master builder of Paris cathedral; he separated the double side aisles by a row of supports consisting of smooth columns with base and capital, and made up of column
drums, alternating with corresponding columns loosely encircled by smaller, post-
like slim colonnettes. These 12 colonnettes have bell-shaped foliate capitals, each
collected together in a joint high impost via the two columns in the four axes, and
placed at an angle and slightly back from the diagonally arranged columns. In
around 1205/1210 this column form was taken up again in the choir ambulatory of
the Victorine abbey of Saint-Jean in Sens (octagonal pillar with alternating full and
half columns).

In the same way, in around 1170, the master builder of the cathedral of Laon
emphasised the alternating vertical supports in the sexpartite vaulted nave by
encircling the second and fourth round columns, each with a capital and made up of
column drums, with five smaller free-standing columns. Their monolithic shafts are

divided in the middle by shaft rings (annulets), and their bud capitals do not reach even half the height of those of the 'main columns'. Their bases are also lower. In the nave of the cathedral of Lincoln (c. 1220/1230) and in the choirs of the cathedrals of Chichester (between 1187 and 1210) and Salisbury (after 1220) the master builders surrounded the polygonal pillar core with four or eight smaller columns of Purbeck marble, which match the lines of the vaulting. This was seen previously in Canterbury in 1177. Soon after 1220, in the description of the life of Hugo I, Bishop of Lincoln, the round pillars in the choir of Lincoln cathedral, built 1192–1200 and surrounded by half-height pillars with shaft rings, are described as 'little columns, that are surrounded by columns in such a way that they seem to be dancing a kind of roundelay'.

From these observations we can conclude that in the 1180s and 1190s in France and England the octagonal or round supports made up of drums and having a base and a capital were no longer described as columns, but as pillars (Gervase calls them accordingly *pilarii*). As such they could be furnished with colonnettes, as in the case of traditional pillars. Taking this formal background and development into account, the supports in the nave of Chartres cathedral (c. 1200/1210) must therefore be regarded as pillars with round or octagonal shafts. They are derived from round or polygonal half-columns, the shafts of which are made out of uniform layers of blocks, as is also the body of the pillar. The uniqueness of the models becomes clear in that the model for the central nave, which has no structural function at the level of the column capitals, also has no capital at this point; only the impost, which is a concluding element in both pillar and column, was offset above the shaft.

Pier development in the arcades of the nave
In Paris cathedral, built from east to west, the piers first used were of the traditional round shape with a capital from which sprang the arcades and vaulting shafts. On the west side, in around 1210/1220, the vaulting shafts were carried down past the capitals to the floor. In the last bay (as in Chartres and Reims) projections were added around the circumference of the piers to take the graduated arches of the arcade – the development of the Gothic compound pier.

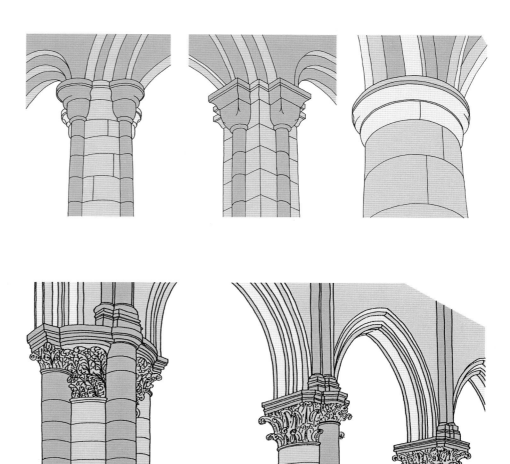

The supports in the nave of Chartres are a continuation of the design of the choir. In the choir ambulatory there is also this change from round to octagonal shafts, including bases: in addition there are octagonal columns on the outer walls. The capitals and the imposts are similar to those of the supports in the nave. Here, too, it is clear that in the case of the so-called *pilier cantonné* in the nave of Chartres the forms of Laon are continued and further developed, evidenced by the small columns projecting from the round core column which here appear as half-columns, and, as in Canterbury cathedral, by the fully implemented alternation of round and octagonal pillars with capitals in the nave. The same logic then applies to the combination of round shaft with octagonal models and vice versa. The almost classical logical consistency of form, typical of the whole building, is therefore also to be found in the structural supports.

The Gothic master builders' understanding of form is particularly clear in the example of the two western bays of the central nave of the cathedral of Paris. The fourth master builder, from 1210/1220, had first placed a three-quarter column facing the central nave projecting from the non-tapering round masonry pillars with capital in the penultimate pair of columns towards the west; this three-quarter column was intended to take the vaulting shafts. Then for the westernmost pair of columns he adopted the style used in Chartres, including the vaulting shaft, without capital, facing the central nave. This column form in Paris is unusual in another way, in that we can trace in it the master builder's thinking on structural design. While the round pillars are made up of individual masonry drums, the shaft of the column in front is monolithic, as it is in part in Reims. In the western column, then,

Round pier with ring of columns
In Chichester cathedral, following a fire in 1187, the piers of the nave were rebuilt as capitalled round piers ringed with free-standing columns of Purbeck marble.

as in Chartres, round pillars and column projections are built up of uniform layers of blocks joined together, in other words the independent components are linked into a single pillar. In Reims this step then had consequences for the capital zone.

The cathedral of Reims is not only of great significance for the development of Gothic sculpture, for progress in building technology and the introduction of tracery windows; it also marks a revolutionary step forward in the development of the column-like pillar with projecting colonnettes into a single unified structural member. In the choir, in the transept and in the six eastern bays of the nave, which were created between 1211 and 1233, all the arcade supports are formed in the same way: projecting from each of the round masonry pillars with capital are half-columns partly built in *en délit* technique (monolithic shafts), with decorated tops that reach the height of the capital of the main column. The capitals of the half-columns, however, are clearly divided between an upper part decorated, as in the main capital, as a bell capital with circles of leaves rolled into crockets, and a lower part, cylindrical in shape and a continuation of the column shaft, decorated with foliate ornamentation or animals.

Despite these differences in design the whole capital zone presents a unified look. The two western column pairs in the nave, which were erected after the interruption to building works between 1233 and 1236, show the final step towards uniting the capitals of the projecting colonnettes with the main capital, in that the wreath of leaves is continued uniformly over the capitals at the same height: abacus and impost merge into a single, narrow head piece which gathers together the round, thicker column core and the projecting colonnettes into a compound support. Thus was created the membered (or compound) pier.

How influential and advanced the design of the columns in Reims was, can be seen in the cathedral of Amiens. Here, as in the choir of the cathedral of Tours (before 1233), which was built at the same time, the height of the capitals is still related to the cross-section of the column; there is also a clear distinction between impost and abacus, both of which are offset all the way round on all capitals. This formation corresponds largely to the western bay in the nave of Paris cathedral. In the nave of the cathedral of Nevers (1220/1230) the main capital and the capitals of the projecting columns are brought together in a unified, relatively low, wreathed capital. The colonnette in the central nave, however, rises without interruption to the capital from which spring the ribs of the vault.

Page 97
Bundle piers in Cologne cathedral
A bundle pier consists of a central pier, from which project vaulting shafts in two thicknesses which take the vault ribs; the pier in the centre is barely visible here; the capitals form a unified, ring-like structure around the whole.

Nave wall of the cathedral of Chartres
In the nave of Chartres cathedral (1194–1220) the round piers are surrounded by octagonal vaulting shafts, and the octagonal piers by round ones; these shafts carry the transverse ribs of the quadripartite vault in the main part of the nave and in the aisles, as well as the archivolts of the arcades. The capitals vary in size in accordance with the cross-section of the shafts. A row triforium and windows with plate tracery fill the span between the vaulting shafts.

The tendency to unify the design of the capital zone may have been influenced by forms such as were observed in the eastern parts of Bourges cathedral built around 1195–1214. Here slim projecting columns of various thicknesses were placed around a mighty round pillar. This led then to forms such as those found in the Liebfrauenkirche in Trier (after 1235): round pillars with projecting colonnettes, articulated by means of ring shafts and capital-like, impost-style wreaths, and forming a single unit with the clerestory wall. The arcades of the choir polygon (influenced by Bourges) of the cathedral of Le Mans (from 1217, clerestory from 1245) are supported on high bundle piers made up of two thicker and two thinner columns, the capitals of which are at different heights, in accordance with the shaft cross-section. Here, however, the transition to the impost is not in the form of a bell, the square impost instead following the curve of the column. In the nave the thick round column has thin projecting colonnettes with capitals forming a projecting double wreath, formed like a bell and supporting rectangular or bevelled imposts (corresponding to the projections).

In the 1230s in the southern nave of the cathedral of Troyes half-column projections were placed around octagonal pillars, with the column capitals being continued at a unified height over the pillars. The unified form of the membered pier,

Development of the Gothic column

The three illustrations show a comparison between different round piers with vaulting shafts.
Above: Amiens cathedral.
Centre: Piers in the west part of the nave of Reims cathedral. They are a precursor to the ring of capitals seen in the compound pier.
Below: Piers in the east part of the nave of Reims cathedral. Here the smaller capitals (with decorated cylinders) of the vaulting shafts have been adjusted to the height of the main capital.

Cathedral of Bourges

The cathedral of Bourges was begun in around 1195, and the choir finished in 1214. The nave was not completed until the middle of the 13th century. A characteristic feature of Bourges cathedral is its large, high, round piers with projecting, slim vaulting shafts in two thicknesses – an early form of the bundle pier.

Choir ambulatory of the abbey church of Saint-Denis
The monolithic vaulting shafts of the choir ambulatory, built 1140–1144 under Abbot Suger, were replaced by round masonry piers with capitals during a reconstruction of the clerestory with pierced triforium. The new piers have a projecting vaulting shaft on the side facing into the interior.

Page 103
Clerestory of Saint-Denis
The continuous vertical lines of the four-panel tracery, spanning the space between the bundles of vaulting shafts, and the pierced triforium bring the whole surface together into a single glowing tapestry of light. These alterations carried out on the abbey church of Saint-Denis between 1231 and 1282 represent a pinnacle of development in Gothic wall elevations.

which was widespread in the High Gothic, led, through multiplication of the number of colonnettes, to the bundle pier, such as is seen in the choir of Cologne cathedral (1248–1322). The membered pier was only seldom used after 1270.

Tracery – The Key to Illuminated Walls

Tracery is an important formal design element within the development of the Gothic style. The effect variously described as the 'diaphanous quality of the wall' (Hans Jantzen, 1927), the 'extending form' and the 'grille-like design of the wall' (Hans Sedlmayr, 1950), and most particularly the introduction of the optical skeleton construction in around 1200/1220 were only made possible through the emergence of tracery as a space-defining element within the building frame. For the optical negation of the wall as a solid border to a space left no room for the kind of light-bringing, wall-penetrating windows found in the Romanesque style. It is this

Unthinkable – A Cathedral without Colour

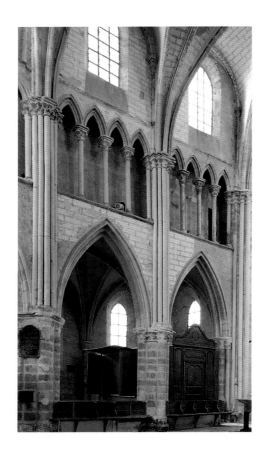

Original coloration of the wall
In the church of the Knights of St John, Saint-Eliphe in Rampillon (Seine-et-Marne), which was built by the Archbishop of Sens from around 1220 to the middle of the 13th century, the original wall articulation is preserved in the way the joints are picked out in colour.

Page 105
Sainte-Chapelle, Paris
The reconstructed colouring, carried out by Eugène E. Viollet-le-Duc in the 19th century, together with the original stained-glass windows of the Sainte-Chapelle (1241–1248), give an impression of the spatial effect intended by its master builder.

Gothic architecture, an artistically designed stone construct, the very expression of masonry art, was originally, at least in the interior and around the portals, plastered, or limewashed, and painted. Today this is difficult to imagine.

Colour and joint painting was intended to bring out the structure of the architectural elements. The remaining non-perforated wall surfaces were painted in colour, such as seen in Rampillon and Marburg, and the rigorous linearity of post-like profiles, vaulting shafts and ribs was alleviated or broken down by means of decorative painting, as in Lausanne and in the Sainte-Chapelle in Paris. In St Elisabeth, Marburg, for example, Jürgen Michler was able to prove that in 1270 the interior had originally been painted all in pink, with the joints marked out in white; on the walls, pillars and vaulting shafts this white marking corresponded largely to the actual jointing pattern, but on the plastered surfaces of the vault the scale was smaller than the underlying one.

The vaulting shafts were painted in the basic pink background colour of the walls and pillars and also covered in joint markings. Ochre and white were the contrast colours used for the transverse arches and the nave arch, but their structure was not broken down by joint painting. In the window tracery the circular moulding was picked out in white on ochre. In the use of colour in the Elisabeth church there is a 'certain ambivalent state brought about by the presence and the veiling of the wall mass. The wall itself has no specific articulation. Quite the reverse in fact. The use of colour emphasises only its surface qualities' (Michler, 1984). The cathedral of Amiens, which was influential in the second phase of building in Marburg, had grey-painted walls and red and ochre vaults in the nave, begun in 1220, these surfaces also having joint markings. The capitals were painted as well, the ornaments being picked out in another colour.

Cloister of the cathedral of Noyon
Classical, four-panel tracery
(c. 1230/1240), as in the clerestory
windows of Amiens and Saint-
Denis, is used here in Noyon to
fill the arcades in the cloister.

change, completed in the choir chapels of the cathedral in Reims in 1215/1220, that above all marks the birth of the true Gothic. Tracery did not replace the lead bars and reinforcement of Romanesque and Early Gothic glass windows, but served as a space-defining grille between the elements of the building's frame. Thus, as a consequence, the tracery forms an entity together with the profiled walls and the accompanying colonnettes supporting vaults; as blind tracery it spans wall surfaces and its profiling corresponds to that common in columns, arches and ribs.

Tracery is built up exclusively of exact circles, and only a pair of compasses and a spirit level were needed to construct it. The wealth of forms found in tracery is practically inexhaustible, giving a variety of designs that is overwhelming. Each individual form is inextricably linked to the next through its geometric location, through the overlapping arcs of circles and through the fixed grid of lines.

The development from closely grouped individual windows to 'group windows' under discharging arches as in Chartres, through finally to the first tracery window in Reims in around 1215/1220, combined with the technical development of tectonically designed wheel and 'punched disc' windows away from architectural members towards the ornamental in the great rose windows, gives rise to a purely genetic explanation which seems more convincing than all other suppositions often proposed in the literature. A striving to 'dissolve' the solidity of the wall was the driving force. Tracery became a structural form, or decoration, at the latest around 1300. This is most impressively demonstrated on the west front of Strasbourg minster where the long, thin tracery bars (only a few centimetres thick), like blue-black silhouettes or the strings of an instrument, are thrown not only in front of the wall surfaces but also in front of the tracery windows.

**Stained-glass windows in
the choir of Saint-Denis**
The chapels around the choir
ambulatory, built 1140–1144 by
Suger, still have their original
stained-glass windows, bathing
the interior of the choir in coloured light, a typical feature
of Gothic architecture.

Pages 108 and 109

Development of the rose window

The wheel and perforated windows in the west front of the cathedral of Chartres, built around 1210/1220 (*page 108, top left*), and in the north transept of Laon, from around 1180/1190 (*page 108, right*), were superseded by tracery in the south transept of the cathedral of Chartres around 1225/1230 (*page 108, middle left*) and in the north transept of Reims around 1230/1240 (*page 108, bottom left*). The west rose of the cathedral of Laon (*page 109*) was added in 1860 as a copy of the rose on the east façade of the choir (1210–1215), in place of a wheel window with inset circular design dating from 1200 of which only fragments still remained.

Tracery consists of vertical, profiled bars (mullions), which may be decorated with round bars of small, slim columns. The bars are of varying thicknesses, divided into the central, dissecting main bars and the thinner, secondary bars. Above the impost line, in the couronnement, is the central part of the tracery, made up of circles, called the foil, and later geometric figures, the leaf and the triskele; these are then enclosed within further circles, and from 1260 onwards curved-sided triangles and squares. The angular shapes at the intersections of the arcs were sometimes finished with thickened nosing cusps, often trifoliate.

The classic style of masonry tracery, typical of the High Gothic (1220–1270), was developed in France; it grew out of the motif of two lancet windows below a circular opening, such as is found in Chartres around 1215, Soissons in 1200/1212, Bourges in 1200/1214 and Reims in 1215/1220. The design consisted of colonnetted mullions above which rise two pointed arches whose apexes merge for a short section with a circle above them, with or without inscribed six-lobed foils (as seen still in the central part of the choir of Saint-Denis from 1231, and in the choir chapels of Beauvais in 1247 where there are eight-lobed foils). Around 1230 at Amiens, Saint-Denis and the Sainte-Chapelle in Paris there emerged the four-panelled tracery window with graduated profiling: the classic articulation of two lancets with circle is repeated in the two lancets. The profile of the window jamb is made up of a sequence of components, the outer ones of which encircle the pointed arches of the window jambs, while the inner ones are led around the main division of the window and received by the main bars. The tracery forms a single unit with the profiled window jamb. As early as around 1250, by stilting the arch bays, there were attempts to achieve a richer decoration even for the narrow, two-panel windows. As in the case

Pages 110 and 111
Saint-Germer-de-Fly near Beauvais
The Lady chapel built after 1259 at the Benedictine monastery of Saint-Germer-de-Fly was dedicated before 1267 by Guillaume de Grez, Bishop of Beauvais. The west wall is dominated by a large rose window. The four-panelled tracery windows are crowned with open-work gablets on the outside; the haunches of these windows, decorated with crockets and finials, intersect with the quatrefoil attic.

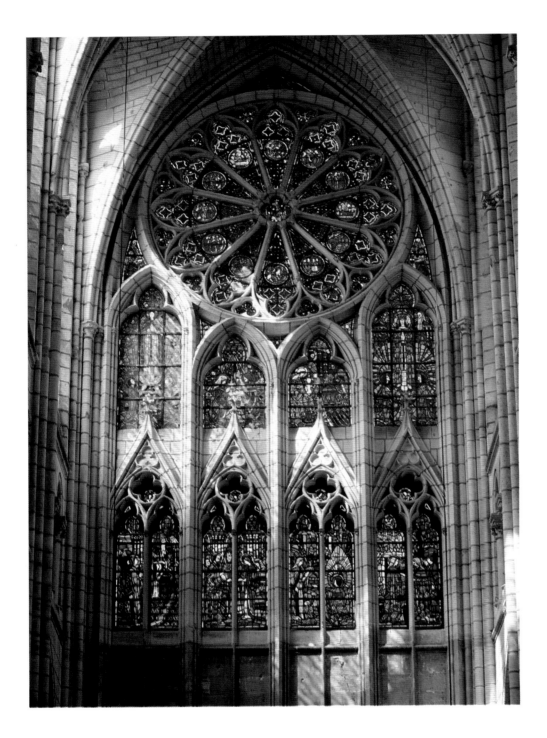

North transept of the cathedral of Soissons

In the 14th century, the rose, four articulated lancet windows and the pierced triforium with tracery and gables were brought together into a unified expanse of glass under the wall rib of the vault – a further development of the north transept of Meaux (1300–1317) and Clermont-Ferrand (1325/1340).

Page 113

South transept of the cathedral of Amiens

The rose and pierced triforium in the south transept of Amiens cathedral (1250–1264) are similar in design to the west wall of Reims (1255–1279), the south transept of Paris (after 1258) and the north transept of the cathedral of Saint-Étienne at Châlons-sur-Marne (from 1256).

of the four-panel windows, smaller three-lobed and four-lobed foils were inserted in circles between the main foil and the lower part. Three unframed trefoils also appeared in the arch bay. In windows with three and six panels the arch bay gets correspondingly larger and more densely filled, with less differentiation between the foils. This can be found in the long choir of Amiens after 1258.

The same development led to the great rose windows seen on west and transept fronts. The windows of the west front of Chartres and of the north transept of Laon – perforated and wheel designs (proven since 1130/1140) – gave inspiration for the creation of geometric circular forms which were then covered with radiating and finally net-like tracery. The dominating influence of the transept façades of Notre-Dame cathedral in Paris (north rose window 1245/1258 under Jean de Chelles, south rose window after 1258 under Pierre de Montreuil) continued until the late 14th century. The removal of the lower spandrel had already been introduced in the north transept of Chartres in 1230, and the enclosing of the rose within a square

while also dispensing with the upper spandrel was then seen in the royal castle chapel of Saint-Germain-en-Laye in around 1238, in Saint-Germer-de-Fly between 1259 and 1267, and later on the north façade of Tours, around 1300. Finally the pointed arch over pierced spandrels was used on the west façade in Reims (1259/1294). The rose is so interlinked with the triforium that a single unified expanse of tracery emerges.

After 1260 the classical design of window tracery tended either towards the addition of a large rose to the couronnement, the rose being made up of many small foils, or towards inserting the foils into the pointed arch form, with trefoils and qua-trefoils making up the majority, and the quatrefoils no longer exclusively in an upright position, but also recumbent. Even earlier, in the Sainte-Chapelle in Paris, the panels were finished with trefoil arches in place of pointed arches. Framing the foils with curved-sided triangles or rectangles in place of circles appeared probably for the first time in the rose window and on the triforium of the south transept, begun in 1258, of the cathedral in Paris. After 1270 this design became quite wide-spread (Narbonne, Toulouse, Évreux, Limoges). Only the churches in central France rejected, until the 14th century, the curved framing; in Tours and Vendôme it was not seen until 1320.

As before in the 13th century, Burgundy and the Champagne region were con-servative about adopting new elements. The lead in the development of tracery was taken by the buildings in the north of the Île-de-France and in Normandy; here is to

Page 115
Angel Choir of Lincoln
Rising above bundle piers with
shaft rings and low foliate capitals
are very wide, richly profiled arcade arches; above these the galleries open into double arcades
below highly graduated discharging arches. The tracery windows
are set back behind a passageway.
In the spandrels are the figures of
angels that give the choir its name.
The vaults bear on black vaulting
shafts made of Purbeck marble, a
popular building material in England; the shafts spring from corbels in the spandrels of the
arcades.

be found the greatest wealth of design and an ever denser pattern, demonstrating beautifully the transformation of an architectural member into an ornament.

In England, in the early years of the Geometric style, 1245–1280, the first tracery windows influenced by Reims and Paris were seen in the new Westminster Abbey. These windows were, however, inserted into the wall plane without reference to the system of vaulting shafts. The design of the four-panel windows in the chapter-house there draws on the windows of the Sainte-Chapelle and those of the choir ambulatory of the cathedral of Paris, both of which were being constructed at the same time. It was not until after 1280 that the window mullions started to be systematically linked with the vaulting shafts. English tracery, modelled on French designs, continued without much change until around 1300, when windows with more panels began to emerge, sometimes as many as eight, as in the Angel Choir of Lincoln cathedral. In the transition to the late Geometric style, three- and four-panel windows appeared in the last quarter of the 13th century. These had a somewhat wider and higher central panel. In front of the mullions were generally colonnettes with base and capital.

The tracery of the last phase of the Geometric style, 1280–1320, was characterised by a general loosening of the classical, French-influenced motifs and a move towards increasing richness through more complex forms, which became softer and were sometimes groined. The result was long-leaved, pointed and framed foil figures, nosed lancet arches or pointed-leaved trefoil arches inside the lancet arches finishing off the individual panels; unframed figures and spandrel motifs became more common. There were also network patterns which arose as a result of arcs crossing and the horizontal or vertical alignment of figures of similar type or size.

In Germany, until 1250, the influence of France was unmistakable. First the classic two-panel window design was taken over from Reims, examples of which can be found in Marburg and Trier, then the four-panel design was also adopted, as in the nave of Strasbourg minster, in the choir of Cologne cathedral and in the Cistercian monastery church of Altenberg. Colonnettes with capital and base and circular moulding were placed in front of the profiles, but simple, flattened groins also occurred, as in Freiburg minster. In the second phase, 1250–1280, there was a transition to richer decorative forms, partly arising in France and partly developing independently in Germany – the circle remained empty or was filled with freely arranged trefoil and quatrefoil figures. Circular moulding was replaced by flattened groins. Full independence was reached in the Strasbourg Façade Elevation B (1275/1278) and the execution of the west building under Erwin of Steinbach († 1318), where a range of new forms was introduced, including the noses on the lancet arches of the panels and the tri-radial figure.

From 1260 onwards unframed foil shapes began to appear, and the first three-panel windows were built: depending on how the couronnements were filled the central panel was raised above the two side panels, as was common in triple window arrangements, or it ended lower, when the central motif fell between the side panels. Six-panel windows were also found, divided either into two sets of three panels, as in the south transept of St Martin in Colmar, or three sets of two panels, as visible in the south transept of the collegiate church of Wimpfen after 1268 and then in Regensburg around 1300. In around 1300 the pendant spandrel form emerged, an early example of which is in Salem in southern Germany.

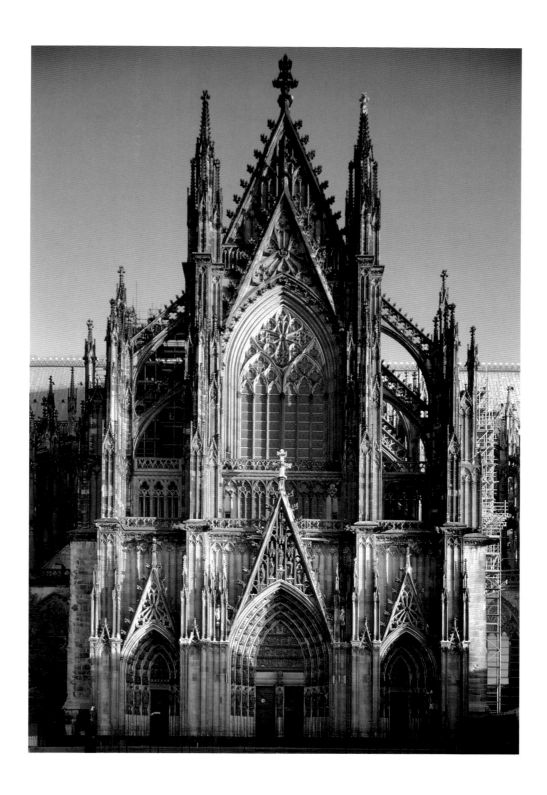

Façade of the south transept of Cologne cathedral

Although planned and begun around 1300 the south transept façade was not built until 1842–1880, when work was completed on the unfinished original building dating from 1560. The figured portals lead into a triple-aisled transept. The openwork gablets of the portals reach up into the next storey in front of the windows of the pierced triforium. Above the large, central tracery window an openwork gablet with associated blind tracery forms the pediment between large finials on the buttresses.

Building the vault on a Gothic cathedral
Reconstruction of the vault of Regensburg cathedral from around 1300, on the basis of an analysis by Manfred Schuller. Wooden arch frames support the flying buttresses, transverse arches and ribs on which the shuttering was laid to carry the vault caps during construction.

Buttresses and Flying Buttresses – Creating an Illusion

The system of buttresses and flying buttresses is an important element in the construction and design of Gothic cathedrals. Together with the transverse arch, cross springers and the vault caps over the nave and side aisles, these elements form an indissoluble unit, and are the key to the stability of the construction. By spanning nave and aisles as a single integrated unit this bay span is quite distinct from the single bays of Romanesque groined vaults, which were used as a simple, regularly repeated spatial element. The Gothic construction system enabled equal-height vaulting to be used across spaces of different sizes by inserting pointed arches, with the legs of the arch being extended at will.

The cross-rib vault collects the reaction and shearing forces mostly via the ribs, the transverse arch and the blind arch and brings them together on four base points, the bearing points of which on the nave wall have to be very well constructed to take the concentrated forces. The wall between the bearing points therefore takes virtually no load and it can be hollowed out, thinned down or completely broken up into tracery windows. As a means of strengthening the wall at the bearing points buttresses are inserted vertically, in line with the distribution of forces, and stepped around the hood-moulding. They project from the wall and together with the projections on the interior wall, the vaulting shafts, they form a structural unit. Examples of this can be found in the choir chapels of the cathedral of Reims, in the Sainte-Chapelle in Paris, in the south transept of the cathedral of Noyon and in Marburg.

The buttresses terminate either in coping which serves as a dripstone and which may be offset with the eaves moulding, or they can be exaggeratedly heightened,

Page 119
Vertical development of the naves of Gothic cathedrals
Cross-sections of naves showing a comparison of the vertical development of Gothic cathedrals from 1170–1300.

1 Noyon, after 1170
2 Paris, 1175–1215
3 Bourges, 1195–1250
4 Chartres, 1194–1220
5 Reims, 1211–1241
6 Amiens, 1220–1230
7 Beauvais, 1227–1260
8 Cologne, 1248–1322

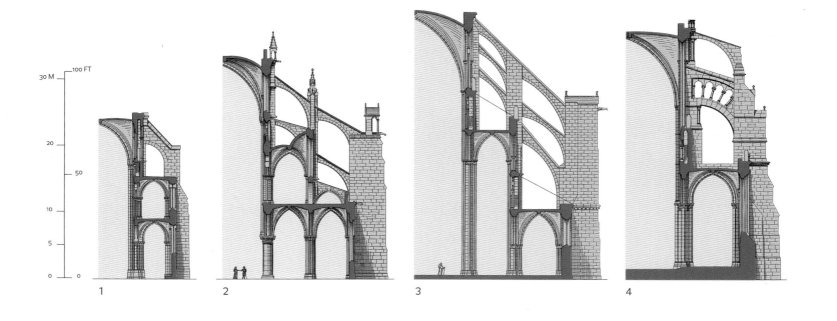

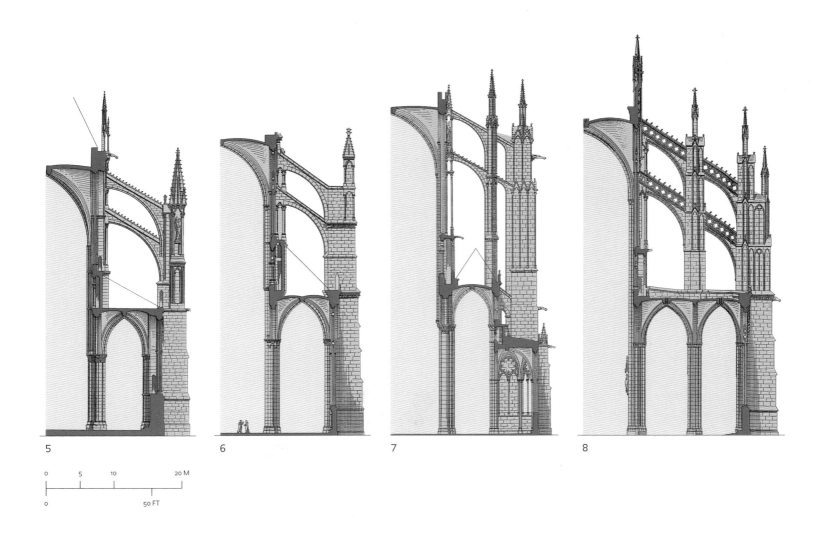

Choir of the cathedral of Notre-Dame, Amiens
View of the south side of the choir with Lady chapel; the choir was begun in around 1236 and the vault added in 1264. Rising above the roofs are clerestory windows between buttresses, from which spring the flying buttresses ending in the clerestory walls.
The openwork gablets of the windows intersect with the eaves.

almost tower-like, with a saddleback roof such as on the choir of the cathedrals of Soissons and Clermont-Ferrand. Alternatively they are crowned with a pinnacle as in Amiens, Bourges, Cologne or the Sainte-Chapelle in Paris, and are decorated with inserted figures such as in the choir of Reims cathedral. In the High Gothic buttresses were additionally faced with tracery, as on the cathedral of Reims and the west façade of Strasbourg minster, and the buttresses extending beyond the eaves moulding were linked with a tracery parapet crowned with pinnacles and interspersed with an openwork gablet. This can be seen in the Sainte-Chapelle in Paris and in Cologne cathedral. The pinnacles and tabernacles are purely decorative forms and serve to give a more open visual impression; only to a very limited extent do they produce the load often ascribed to them, the resultant force of which, from shearing and compression, would make a recognisable alteration.

In order to transfer the vault thrust and the wind pressure on the nave (in the case of a basilica), or on the central part of the choir (in the case of an ambulatory choir), to the outer walls with their buttresses, transverse walls were extended over the transverse arch of the side aisle vaulting, which remains invisible under the slanting roof, as in the cathedral of Durham. This task can also be performed by the vaults of

Buttresses and flying buttresses
A richly articulated buttress system was designed and built around 1260–1264 for the choir vault of Amiens cathedral.

the gallery in the side aisle, like the horizontal flying buttresses in Normandy, the half-tunnel vaults in the Auvergne, the intersecting vaults in Provence, the Île-de-France, Lombardy and the Lower Rhine. The flying buttress, a rising half-arch that directs the vault thrust into the buttresses, stretches to the buttresses above the roofs of the side aisles. It was used from about 1160, first in ambulatory choirs in Normandy and the Île-de-France, such as at Saint-Germain-des-Prés, Saint-Leu-d'Esserent and Saint-Remi in Reims, and from about 1190 also in the nave (as in Paris cathedral), where the discontinuance of the galleries after 1194 in Chartres cathedral led to an intensification of the vertical tendency. For higher naves, and in the case of five-aisled churches, two or three flying buttresses, one above the other, were necessary, as in the cathedral of Bourges.

A flying buttress consists of a self-supporting rising arch, above which is a straight bar or strut. The masonry arch is constructed on a wooden template, with the lower end integrated into the buttress and the upper end springing from the corbel or impost projecting from the clerestory wall. It receives additional support from a colonnette, either engaged in the wall as at Chartres, Soissons, Reims and Le Mans, or standing in front of it, as in the choir of Notre-Dame-en-Vaux in Châlons-sur-Marne, the nave of Amiens, the choir of Clermont-Ferrand, and at Cologne. This arch carries a bar-like strut above it – this strut may be arcaded (as in the choir of the collegiate church of Saint-Quentin in the diocese of Noyon) or it may be made up of two struts separated by quatrefoil tracery (as in Cologne cathedral). The development can be seen very clearly in Noyon, where the flying buttresses consist of two layers of stone, one above the other, and in Chartres, where the arch is formed from a single, mighty layer, placed on end. Later the internal construction of the flying buttresses could be derived from the joints that clearly separate the load-bearing arch from the struts (Bourges, Clermont-Ferrand). In terms of construction a flying buttress is an arch plus a strut. It may be pierced by small arcades or tracery (flying arcade, tracery bridge; choir of the cathedral of Amiens) and is covered with a slab or with saddle-backed coping. Crocket decoration is sometimes also used.

In the case of double flying buttresses the lower one serves to take the vault thrust, the upper one wind forces. In Chartres the wind forces had clearly been underestimated, as it became necessary to build several more flying buttresses above the original ones. An important aspect in the flying buttress is its angle of inclination, because a gently sloping strut produces more unfavourable loading on the buttresses than a steeper one. However, the steeper the angle at which the upper strut meets the clerestory wall, the greater is the load required from the roof and the roof covering to balance out the 'upload' from the strut. In terms of the progress of construction work this meant that the roof had to be built before attaching the flying buttress between the clerestory and the buttress. Both the flying buttress and the vault had to be added at the same time to avoid one-sided pressure on the clerestory wall. Constructing the roof before the vault gave the advantage that the roof frame could be used as a working platform for erecting the vault. In 1220/1230 Villard de Honnecourt's elevations of the wall between the central part of the nave and the side aisles in Reims showed this situation quite clearly: the vault is not yet constructed on the inside, nor are the flying buttresses on the outside; only the wall brackets and the bearing points on the buttresses are seen as preparations for the next stage. It should be pointed out, however, that the buttress construction illustrated by him was not in fact carried out in this form in 1230/1240.

Initially this buttress system was a purely functional element, but it gradually turned into an art form and became a dominating characteristic in the exterior design of Gothic cathedrals. The heavy, wide buttresses on the nave walls of Chartres (1194–1210) advanced into bold, narrow pillars with double flying buttresses on the choir of Chartres (1210/1220) and at Bourges (1209–1214). This development culminated in the choir of Beauvais (1227–1272) where the almost post-like buttresses, reaching 50 m in height, and the flying buttresses together form a space-enclosing shell around the cathedral. Simpler constructions, as found particularly in Burgundy, had an influence in Germany around 1210/1220, as evidenced by the cathedral of Limburg, the decagon of St Gereon in Cologne, the nave of Bonn minster and, from 1235, the churches in Marburg and Trier.

The technical construction of Gothic cathedrals, which can be observed particularly well in the buttress system, was based on the experience of the builders and their understanding of the distribution of forces. The structures we see in a Gothic cathedral are, in fact, merely supplementary to the actual supporting structure, which remains largely invisible. The lines traced out by the ribs and the vaulting shafts give only an optical impression, for they are not the elements which actually support the vaults and the perforated tracery-and-light walls. This function is performed instead by the vault caps and the pillars behind the vaulting shafts, in conjunction with the wall arches linking them and the outer buttress system. The architecture we see is an illusion!

The geometric principle of order and design was the key factor leading inevitably to complicated constructions, hidden away from sight, for safely taking up

Page 123

Flying buttress with tracery bridge
On the choir of Amiens cathedral (vaulted in 1264), the arch and tracery bridge of the flying buttresses support the diagonals which direct vault and wind pressure down from the clerestory into the buttresses. This arrangement, together with the buttresses, richly decorated with blind tracery and crowned with finials, creates a graceful three-dimensional openwork structure around the outside of the church.

**Double flying buttresses
at Chartres**
Before 1220 a sequence of lancets
was built on to an arch of the choir
of Chartres cathedral to take the
actual diagonal struts. After this
was done, or perhaps as a result of
a change of plan, a second flying
buttress was added on top, which
was designed to direct the wind-
loading from the eaves on to the
roof.

and distributing loads and forces. This principle is also the one which replaced the
Romanesque 'body-and-space' effect. The cross-rib vault with its ribs marking out
the line of forces was one of the ideal elements in the design. In this way the construction technique used in Romanesque building from about 1100 was adopted for
Gothic cathedrals and integrated into a linear unit with the design of the high nave
by means of the vaulting shafts. It was not the introduction of the cross-rib vault and
the pointed arch that characterised the Gothic, it was instead the design benefits
provided by cross-rib vaults and pointed arches that prompted the Gothic master
builders to choose these forms.

Moreover the Gothic cathedral is not a skeleton construction in the sense of
19th-century iron and steel architecture, but is most definitely a follow-on from the
Romanesque tradition of vertical, articulated masonry structures. In the Gothic,
however, the wall mass was reduced as far as possible and its optical effect coun-
teracted by geometrically based articulating elements worked by stonemasons.

50-m high buttress system
Maximum vertical and minimum horizontal development of a buttress is shown in the choir of the cathedral of Beauvais, which was started after a fire in 1225 and completed, with the choir ambulatory, around 1245. The upper storeys and the vault with buttress system were built in 1255–1272. In 1284 parts of the nave collapsed because the span of this high structure was too wide (rebuilt by 1324).

Modern structural calculations and the experience gained from repairing and strengthening Gothic cathedrals have made it clear that they were not skeleton constructions with infill sections, but only appeared to be so. The Gothic master builders used all the design and construction means at their disposal to achieve this effect, while at the same time also mastering perfectly the distribution of forces, as proven by the stability of the buildings they created.

The Triforium – A Wall Passage at Dizzy Heights

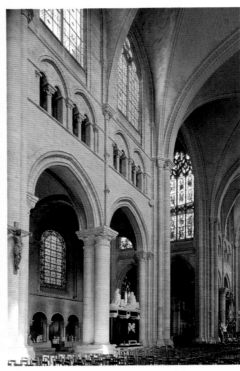

Articulation of the Early Gothic nave wall

Left: The cathedral of Noyon (begun in 1150) shows the traditional quadripartite wall elevation with arcade, gallery, row triforium and clerestory windows; the sexpartite rib vault above the square bays of the nave dictates the alternating column design.
Right: The Archbishop's cathedral of Saint-Étienne in Sens, built 1140–1168, also has an Early Gothic sexpartite vault, without a gallery but with a triforium which opens into the roof space of the aisles. (The windows of the clerestory were enlarged after 1268.)

The triforium is a passage within the wall between the arcades or the gallery and the window zone of a basilica, at the level of the sloping roof over the side aisles. It is open to the nave via either arcades or tracery. The triforium is of special significance for the articulation of the upper part of the wall between the nave and the side aisles in Gothic churches. This feature began to emerge around the middle of the 12th century (for example the cathedral in Sens around 1160); the connection between the open triforium and the clerestory, as in Saint-Denis from 1231, led finally to the abandonment of the triforium and the classic three-tier construction of the wall. The first mention of the word triforium came in 1185 from Gervase of Canterbury writing about the wall passage in the choir of Canterbury cathedral: '... above this wall was a walkway [wall passage], which is called a triforium' (*supra quem murum via erat, quae triforium appellatur*). Villard de Honnecourt made a drawing in 1220/1230 of the triforium in Reims and described it as *voies*, in other words 'ambulatories'.

Various types of opening to the nave can be distinguished. One variant is the 'row triforium' spanning the distance from vaulting shaft to vaulting shaft. Examples of this model, which was developed in Burgundy on the basis of motifs from classical architecture, can be seen in Chartres, Reims, Laon, Braine, Noyon and Notre-Dame-en-Vaux in Châlons-sur-Marne. A second type is the 'group triforium', established in Normandy, in which the twin or triple arcades, mostly coupled under a blind arch, were cut into the wall, as for example in Sens, Amiens, Bourges, Beauvais, Westminster Abbey, Canterbury and York. And finally, after 1230, in the case of the 'pierced triforium' the tracery of the windows was extended down to the triforium sill and this, in combination with the window openings in the rear wall of the triforium, created a continuous area of light, such as exemplified in Saint-Denis, Troyes, Strasbourg, Amiens, Cologne and Beauvais.

The triforium can be found in the nave, the transept and the choir, predominantly in France around 1150–1300. In the region around Cologne and Basle it was constructed between 1200 and 1260, with only a few examples occurring in Westphalia, Holland, Nuremberg, Assisi and Roskilde (Denmark). The forerunners of the triforium were found in the form of niche articulation in the wall zone over the arcades in the 11th century in the Rhineland, in rectangular, wheel-shaped or arcade openings to the roof space in the Île-de-France and in the Rhine-Meuse area in the first half of the 12th century, and in the blind articulation in Normandy and Burgundy around 1100.

The triforium can be constructed in a number of different ways. A wall passage may be built between the rear wall and the arcades below a masonry arch spanning the gap from vaulting shaft to vaulting shaft; the passageway is not continued under the vaulting shafts and each section is accessible from the roof of the side aisle. In place of the arch the wall passage may also be covered by stone slabs or a longitudinal barrel vault and continued behind the vaulting shafts. Another type of construction is to place the rear wall of the triforium on the vault over the aisle, or on a discharging arch projecting from the wall over the side aisles. This type is described as a 'box triforium'. Alternatively the rear wall of the triforium is fitted with windows (which enables hipped roofs over the side aisles), this form being described as a 'pierced triforium'.

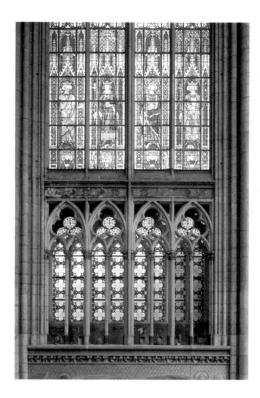

Triforium and window tracery create a unified light effect
In the nave of Cologne cathedral the pierced triforium and the tracery in the high clerestory windows together create a single, unified plane of coloured light.

Articulation of the clerestory in Lichfield
In the nave of Lichfield cathedral (second half of the 13th century), the triforium opens as a dark zone in the double profiled arches with inset tracery lancets, above which are low clerestory windows.

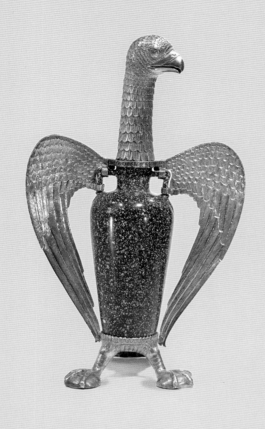

DEVELOPMENTS IN FRANCE

Classic Gothic Cathedrals

Page 129
Porphyry vase with eagle
This vase of porphyry was made at the time of Abbot Suger in around 1140. Originally in the treasury at Saint-Denis, it can now be seen in the Louvre in Paris.

There is no general agreement about the exact date the Gothic style began in France, even though 1140, when work started on the choir of Saint-Denis, is often quoted as the year of its birth. Hans Erich Kubach, probably the most knowledgeable authority on Romanesque architecture in France and Germany, said in 1977 in a catalogue for the exhibition *Die Zeit der Staufer* (The Era of the Hohenstaufen): 'In France, from about 1140 onwards, many different tendencies converge, resulting in greater and greater standardisation in church building and in increasing structuring of the building form. Yet, until the end of 1200, this development remained so closely linked with its Romanesque origins that it can be described as Late Romanesque.' From the point of view of the Romanesque style this is correct. But from the point of view of the fully developed Gothic it is also justifiable to regard this phase with Saint-Denis and Laon as a first step in the development towards the style of Gothic that reached its full expression around 1190 in Chartres with the triple-layered wall elevation, quadripartite rib vault, buttress system, extensive tracery panels and round pillars with capitals and projections. This, in turn, can be understood as simply a further step on the road to the classical Gothic period, as expressed in 1211/1233 in Reims cathedral with its tracery, membered pillars and series production of standardised building elements on the basis of construction plans. This stage reached its full peak of development between 1231 and 1245 with the complete breaking down of the wall and illumination of the interior, as shown in the examples of Saint-Denis, the Sainte-Chapelle in Paris and, from 1255/1272, in the choir of Beauvais cathedral.

As in all fields of history, art and architecture, too, is not about events, about suddenly coming into existence, emerging spontaneously with no models or influences from earlier motifs; it is instead about processes which have neither a fixed starting point nor a fixed end, but which merge into one another, growing out of a declining process, building upon it or starting out in a new direction. On the other hand it is quite possible that at different locations, independent of each other, the same or similar processes may develop, given related or identical formal or intellectual investigation. And these processes can lead to related forms and designs and may indeed be stylistically identical. If we look at building developments in France between 1140 and 1300, we can identify four stages of innovation, linked to the individual buildings in the Île-de-France: first the choir of Saint-Denis and the cathedral of Laon, secondly Chartres, thirdly Reims and fourthly the rebuilding of Saint-Denis and the Sainte-Chapelle in Paris.

The Early Gothic

The first buildings with Gothic forms began to emerge in the 1130s, with the cathedral of Saint-Étienne in Sens, under Archbishop Henri de Sanglier († 1142), and with the western building and the choir of the abbey church of Saint-Denis under Abbot Suger. The growing political and economic significance of the French kingdom under the Capetians, whose position was closely linked to the papacy, brought a

A Gothic building site
The scene in a window at the Sainte-Chapelle in Paris shows two masons and a labourer at work. The man on the right is using a trowel to divide up mortar while the one in the middle takes the material up to the working level using a V-shaped wooden hod carried on two poles across his shoulders. The mason on the left of the picture is laying bricks.

Pages 132 and 133
Cathedral of the Archbishop of Sens
West and north elevation of the nave of the cathedral of Saint-Étienne in Sens, begun around 1140 and almost completed by 1168. The westwork was built gradually after the town fire of 1184, the chapels on the first upper storey were dedicated in 1210 and 1221. The clerestory windows were enlarged after the fire of 1268.

new artistic focus to architecture in the Île-de-France. This consisted of linking the Norman cross-rib vaulted basilicas from the first quarter of the 12th century, as exemplified in Durham, Winchester, Peterborough, Gloucester, Lessay, Duclair and Saint-Paul in Rouen, with the pointed arch from Burgundy, as found for example in Paray-le-Monial, Autun and Cluny.

While the oldest part of the cathedral of Sens, the choir ambulatory, dating from the 1130s, still had a round arch, just three decades later pointed arches were used in the central part of the choir and in the nave. The wide transverse arches each comprise two bays which, in the Norman style, enclose a sexpartite vault. The intermediate ribs are taken up by a vaulting shaft which rises above the impost of the round coupled masonry pillars with capitals, seen here for the first time. Between the double bays, the sculptural bundle of vaulting shafts leading down in front of the wall into the floor gives distinct rhythmical emphasis from the nave to the apse. The wall elevation is divided into three tiers: above the arcades are a group triforium and coupled windows in the clerestory without projecting Norman wall passage. In the 13th century the windows here were enlarged.

The special features of Sens become clear in a comparison with a contemporary structure, the abbey church of Saint-Germer-de-Fly, the choir of which was begun in 1132 and finished in 1145. Here pointed arches and buttressed walls were used, but the Norman-style hollowed-out clerestory is retained above a sill cantilevered

on brackets as a wall passage. Here, too, we can see a four-tier construction of the walls – arcades, galleries, rectangular openings to the roof space instead of a triforium, and a clerestory.

Norman westworks such as Sainte-Trinité in Caen were influential in the design of the westwork of the abbey church of Saint-Denis near Paris, a twin-towered, much restored structure standing in front of the Carolingian basilica. Yet the towers, articulated only by buttresses, took on an individual aspect through the disappearance of the horizontal cornice across the front. After the consecration of the westwork in 1140 Abbot Suger erected the new choir above the old crypt, which he had enlarged so that it could carry the double choir ambulatory with radiating chapels. The ambulatory could have been constructed in different ways: The semicircular chapels, between which on the outside deep buttresses were placed, merged in the interior with the outer choir ambulatory, or a second ambulatory was created, taking into account the five-part rib vault, by opening the side walls of the chapels. The pointed-arch ribs, transverse arch and nave arch with simple round profile, as in Notre-Dame in Morienval and Saint-Étienne in Beauvais, were supported by slim columns with monolithic, non-tapering shafts. What emerged was a free, light hall space, embracing the central part of the choir like a ring of light by means of the two large windows in each of the shallow-bayed chapel niches. In his writings about the consecration celebrations on 11 June 1144, Suger made particular note of this effect. After 1231 the columns and the superstructure of the central part of the choir were rebuilt, together with the transept and the nave.

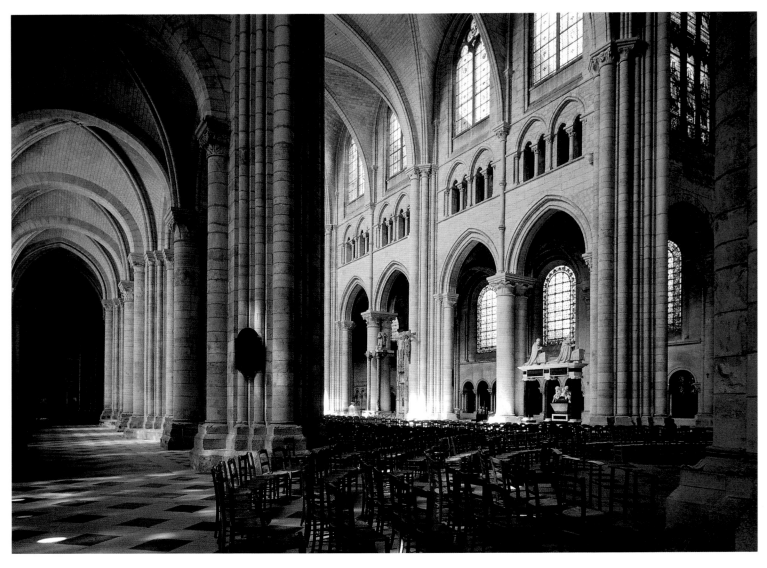

Pages 134 and 135
Interior view of the cathedral of Sens
The sexpartite vault above square bays was erected 1140–1168. The triforium opens into the roof space above the aisles. The windows were enlarged after 1268.

Emerging at the same time as the buildings in the Île-de-France was a separate development in Maine, Poitou and Anjou, using pointed arches and cambered vaults, such as are seen in the reconstruction of the nave of the cathedral of Saint-Julien in Le Mans after 1135 and in the triple-span hall churches with cambered rib vaults of the cathedrals of Angers and Poitiers. These territories further south had become part of the Anglo-Norman lands of the Plantagenets following the marriage of the heir to the English throne, later Henry II, to Eleanor of Aquitaine in 1152. Henry and Eleanor ordered the building of Poitiers cathedral in 1162, and it was completed in the 1180s. The transverse, nave and blind arches are shaped, like the ribs, as narrow roll moulding and rest on a row of evenly placed round columns, as in Laon and Paris. In the 13th century, in the choir of the abbey church of Saint-Serge in Angers, the thin-ribbed vaults were set on extremely slim columns, forming a light and open space connecting to the hall nave on square pillars with semicircular

Pages 136 and 137
Bishop's palace at Sens
The bishop's palace, *salle synodale,*
was built in around 1235/1240 and
restored in the 19th century by
Viollet-le-Duc. The building has
rich fenestration: two double windows under a large oculus in a
pointed arch and echoes of the
tracery found on the cathedral
windows. The buttresses are
crowned with figures in tabernacles and linked at eaves level
with a crenellated gallery.

projections. The cambered vaults remained a characteristic feature of the spatial
impression, as for example in the six western bays in the cathedral of Poitiers, at Air-
vault, Candes and Asnières.

In northern France stylistic development concentrated on the elevation of the
basilical central nave wall and the choir wall. In the second half of the 12th century
attempts were made to create a kind of articulated framework in front of an ever
more 'broken down' wall, the structural equivalent of an optical framework of lines
in front of a differentiated spatial background. This is illustrated well in the north
and south conches of the cathedral of Noyon, which were built one after the other
in the 1160s and restored in 1914/1918.

Here, in front of the wall, is a veritable 'scaffolding' of shafts and ribs. The wall
itself is divided into four distinct zones: a lower section with blind pointed arches,
above this a three-part row triforium, then a second, very high triforium with double arcades discharging in pointed arches, and, high in the vaulting, double lancet
windows, separated by rod-like members and connecting directly to the ribs without a section of wall between. The upper zone is flooded with light and it also illu-
minates the galleries. What results is a kind of optical dissolution of the wall space,
increasing in effect towards the top; the wall space is interrupted by the shafts
above which the mouldings separating the different levels are offset, so that the
space-forming wall foil and the system of articulation are linked and the horizontal
and vertical systems merge together and balance one another out.

Pages 138 and 139

The abbey church with the kings' tombs

Abbot Suger of Saint-Denis was responsible for the restoration of the venerable Merovingian church. Work progressed in several stages: 1135–1140, the twin-towered westwork (only one tower now stands) with chapels in the upper storey was built; and 1140–1144 the choir with ambulatory and radiating chapels was added. The transept wing and aisles begun after this were not completed until the restoration of the choir clerestory in 1231–1245.

West façade of the cathedral of Noyon
The twin-towered west façade was built in around 1220–1231, after work was completed on the nave. It bears the influence of the west façades of Saint-Denis (1140) and Laon (1190–1205).

Cathedral of Noyon
View of the cathedral from the north, showing the choir and the east wing of the cloister.

Transept and nave, Noyon
Following a fire in 1131, work on the cathedral of Noyon progressed slowly. The choir was completed in 1157 and the transept in 1160–1170; the nave was started around 1170 and probably finished by around 1200. A quadripartite wall elevation is evident in the nave: arcades separating the aisle, gallery, row triforium, pairs of clerestory windows under the wall ribs, and above that a sexpartite rib vault which dictates the alternation of piers with vaulting shafts and column-like round piers with capitals.

Early Gothic cathedral
View from the nave to the choir of the cathedral of Noyon, begun after 1131 and completed around 1200. The main space, comprising nave, crossing and central part of the choir, is surrounded by further spatial zones (aisles, gallery) and walls with spatial depth (triforium). Attention is directed towards the altar, which is brightly lit by the large windows.

In the south conch, completed only a little later, windows were added to the lower level, above the blind arcades, in such a way that only the triforium forms a dark zone. After 1170 the articulation of the choir (built by 1157) was taken up in the nave; in place of the blind triforium, however, was the row triforium of the transept conches, now in the traditional position underneath the windows – the design of which now follows that of the windows of the conches. The sexpartite rib vault is gathered into the shafts which end on the intermediate round masonry pillars with capitals, which themselves lead down to the floor on the pillars carrying the transverse arch.

The elements used in this architecture come from the repertoire of forms of the Romanesque period, and all were available to the Gothic. The double-skin wall was also found in the apses of older churches such as Saint-Nicolas (1083–1093) and Sainte-Trinité (c. 1100) in Caen, in Cérisy-la-Forêt and in English churches such as the cathedral of Peterborough (1118–1140). The rib vault, too, was common in Norman architecture in northern France – in Caen, Saint-Étienne and Sainte-Trinité in 1110/1120 – and in England, for example in the choir of Durham cathedral 1093–1110. The same is true of the quadripartite wall elevation used in the cathedrals of Tournai (nave begun c. 1135/1140) and St Donatus in Bruges (c. 1130) and in English architecture at the time. This kind of wall elevation was also taken up in the middle of the 12th century in Noyon, Cambrai, Saint-Germer-de-Fly, Laon, Paris and in the 1170s and 1180s in Saint-Remi in Reims and Notre-Dame-en-Vaux in Châlons-sur-Marne.

Cathedral of Noyon

View from the choir of the cathedral (after 1131–1157) looking west to the main entrance, which was only opened for processions on special feast days.

The gallery at Noyon

The gallery opens through wide arches to the crossing, with a view of the nave, transept and choir. The cross-rib vault rests on vaulting shafts with rich foliate capitals. The high round-arched windows, covering almost all the wall space, as yet have no tracery.

Pages 144 and 145
Westwork of the cathedral of Laon
The west front of the cathedral of
Laon (1180/1190–1205, towers
later) was built in the Norman-
Early Gothic architectural tradition. Between the buttresses and
in front of the three portals are
deep, barrel-vaulted vestibules.
They end in gables between which
pinnacles rise up to intersect with
the window zone and the cornice
moulding between the storeys.
A large round window (the tracery
has been replaced) extends above
the deeply stepped side windows.
Both the moulding and even the
dwarf gallery above are also
stepped accordingly. Tabernacle
pinnacles lead to the open storeys
of the towers, which are transformed into octagons through the
angled corners. Standing on the
projections thus formed are monumental, two-storey tabernacles,
square at first then becoming
octagonal, which frame a very narrow, pointed-arched lancet opening with stepped reveal.

The Cathedral of Laon

The pre-Romanesque cathedral of Laon had already been burned down and rebuilt
when Gautier de Mortagne († 1174) became bishop in 1155. In the 1160s he ordered
new building work to begin, initially concentrating on erecting a square, double-
bay choir with apse and ambulatory. In the 1180s the triple-span transept with large
round perforated windows was erected between two flanking towers on each
transept front, and also the projecting apses on the east towers; the nave was
extended as far as a fifth bay, this work being completed around 1190. Further building, in the years up to 1205, comprised the west part of the nave and the west twin-
towered front with three deep vestibules in front of the stepped portals with figural
decoration. Between 1205 and 1215 the choir and apse were replaced by a seven-
bay, triple-span choir with a flatter end in continuation of the nave; dominating the
east wall of this new choir were three mighty lancet windows under a large round
window with tracery.

The arcades on round masonry pillars with capitals, the gallery and the row triforium extend around the transept arms, as do a sequence of simple large windows
set back and framed with columns. The sexpartite vault rests on shaft bundles,
richly decorated with shaft rings, above which the horizontal moulding is offset.
The alternating sequence of three or five shafts, a factor of the vaulting, was reflected in the six small columns placed around the round pillars in the two east double bays; this sequence, however, gave way to an even row of round masonry pillars
with capitals. Thus the effect of individual bays is removed.

Barrel-vaulted vestibules stand between the mighty projecting buttresses in
front of the three portals. The vestibules end in low-pitched gables between which
'grow' tabernacles. The west wall of the nave, also enclosed between the two towers, is dominated by a large round window, but nothing is now known about the

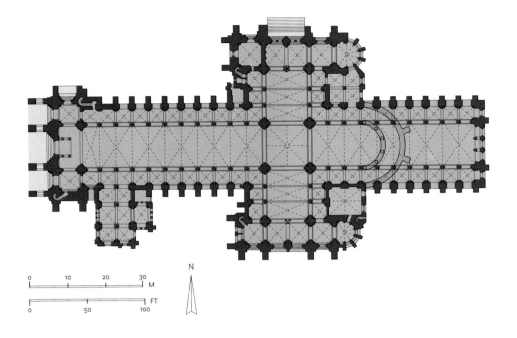

Pages 146 and 147

**Ground plan, nave and crossing of
the cathedral of Laon**
The transept and nave of the
cathedral of Laon were built in
the 1180s. Their characteristic
features are: arcades on compact
round masonry piers with capitals;
deep galleries opening through
double arcades below discharging
arches; row triforium; and large
windows in reveals framed with
columns. The sexpartite vault
rests on bundles of vaulting shafts
decorated with many shaft rings
and angled around the horizontal
moulding.

Lady chapel in the north transept of Laon
In the northeast corner of the north transept of the cathedral of Laon is a Lady chapel which was built around 1160/1180. Large windows illuminate the space.

design of the original window here – whether it was a perforated or wheel window. The tracery window seen today in this position is a modern copy of the later window in the east choir. The two square towers rise up above a stilted round-arched gallery, crowned with tabernacles. The corners of the square towers are bevelled to produce an octagon. Monumental double-height tabernacles are raised on these angles, starting out square and becoming octagonal. These tabernacles frame a very narrow, pointed-arched lancet opening with stepped jamb. In around 1220/1230 Villard de Honnecourt praised these towers, with their appealing sculptures of oxen, as the most beautiful he had ever seen, and drew accurate plans and elevations of them. Bamberg and Naumburg took their inspiration from Laon. Laon was very influential, too, in the Champagne and in Lorraine, and also in the design of Limburg cathedral and the choir of the abbey church of Sainte-Madeleine in Vézelay, the latter, however, having no triforium.

Laon, which today has five towers, is supposed originally to have had seven – two each on the west front, one on each corner of the transept gable and a crossing tower. Eight were originally planned for Chartres and as many as ten for Reims, but they were never carried out in such numbers, as the enthusiasm for further building waned after the churches started to be used. The northwest tower of Chartres is the oldest steeple in France; it is not known what the final design of the top of the towers in Laon was intended to be. Paris did not opt for a large number of towers, stopping at just the two on the west front. In Reims a development started, ending with the building of Amiens, whereby the square towers were reduced to flat, 'show' fronts only on the west elevations. In Amiens the individual features were no longer carried around on to the sides.

Above and below

Crossing and sexpartite vault

View of the crossing of the cathedral of Laon (around 1180) with the open, illuminated crossing tower finished with an eight-part rib vault. A sexpartite rib vault spans the nave like an umbrella above the arcades, galleries and triforium of the nave. Large round-arched windows on either side of the nave illuminate the space.

The double aisles (built around 1180/1190) of Notre-Dame cathedral in Paris are separated by richly profiled arches. They rest on round piers surrounded by colonnettes, similar to those in the naves of the cathedrals of Laon and Chichester (see page 96) – a precursor of the Gothic membered or compound pier.

Notre-Dame, Paris
This detail shows a part of the tympanum of the south portal of the cathedral of Paris, bearing scenes from the life of Saint Stephen, who was the original patron of the cathedral. On the left and in the middle are two scenes of Stephen giving a sermon, on the right is his trial before the council, as described in the story of the Apostles in the New Testament (Acts, 6 and 7). At the bottom of the picture, part of the figure of Stephen can still be seen on the trumeau.

Notre-Dame, Paris

As originally used in Laon, the choir in the cathedral of Notre-Dame in Paris also took up the idea of a choir with ambulatory, but as a double formation, thus leading the double side aisles around the choir. This unified design is hardly interrupted by the transept arms, which initially did not project. King Louis VII, who had been educated at the cathedral school, donated 200 livres to the fund for the new building. But this sum was in no way enough. Bishop Maurice de Sully, who instigated the new building, had 'built the church, a highly appropriate and complicated structure, more with his own means than from monies supplied by others', as reported by his successor Sigebert de Gembloux.

The wall elevation in Paris is four-tiered, but instead of a triforium it had a round opening with five-lobed tracery, removed around 1230 at the time the pointed-

Bishop's church, Paris
View of the crossing, choir and north wall of the transept of the cathedral of Notre-Dame in Paris, begun around 1163. The choir was dedicated in 1182, and the nave finished by 1196. In the transept the quadripartite wall elevation was reconstructed by Viollet-le-Duc, as the windows had been enlarged after 1225.

arched clerestory windows cut into the wall were enlarged. In the east bay it was reconstructed by Viollet-le-Duc. The sexpartite vaults in the nave are captured in the west by shafts leading down in front of the round pillars; corresponding semi-circular columns take up the arcade arches. This marks the beginning of the membered pillar so typical of the Gothic (see Chapter 'An Interplay of Forces'). In around 1200 construction work began on the flat, wide west façade, the mighty walls of which are deeply hollowed out by three richly stepped portals. The façade is dominated by a band of statues of the kings of France under the 9.6-m rose window, above which rise the two square towers with delicate arcading.

Saint-Étienne, Bourges

Like the cathedral in Paris, the cathedral of Saint-Étienne in Bourges, started in 1195 at the same time as Chartres, also shows an older-style semicircular choir with double ambulatory, stepped in the upper reaches, and small radiating chapels that project only slightly. By 1214 Mass was already being said in the choir, and in 1218 all building work was completed. Above the arcades in the central part of the choir and above the inner arcades in the ambulatory is a wide triforium with six equal-height arcades under a semicircular discharging arch. Next to this, in the five-aisled nave which was built before 1260, the same three-tier articulation can be seen, in a stepped arrangement in the wall between the central part of the nave and the side aisles, but here the arcades in the triforium are graduated within the arch.

The high, round pillars, projecting from the wall, together with narrow vaulting shafts and a sexpartite rib vault, create a richly differentiated spatial impression, extending from the nave to form a single spatial unit, an independent achievement that is fully comparable to Chartres. It was based on no model, simply influenced by ideas from the Champagne and Soissons. 'None of this, however, explains in the truest sense the visionary art of the master', confirmed Grodecki in 1986. The influence of Bourges was less than that of Chartres. The lower parts of the choir in the cathedrals of Le Mans and Coutances to the north of Caen can be mentioned here, and Burgos in Spain.

The relatively small Premonstratensian monastery church of Saint-Yved in Braine, begun in 1195/1200, finished soon after 1204 and probably consecrated in

Pages 152 and 153
Saint-Étienne, Bourges
Building work started on the cathedral in around 1195, and in 1214 the choir and the two double bays at the east end of the nave were completed. Work on the other bays of the nave and the westwork continued until the middle of the 13th century. The church, erected within a short space of time, gives a good impression of the dominant effect of a Gothic cathedral.

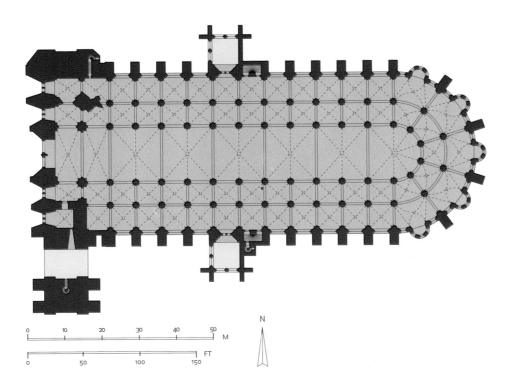

0 10 20 30 40 50 M

0 50 100 150 FT

N

Pages 154 and 155
Large, five-aisled construction
The double aisles of the cathedral
of Saint-Étienne in Bourges, built
from around 1195 to 1250/1260,
continue around the long choir
and apse as a double ambulatory;
between the mighty buttresses
are five small apses. Thick round
piers with thin, projecting vaulting
shafts support the high arcades
and carry the sexpartite rib vault.

1208, is another building which exercised its own influence. In each of the two corners between the choir and the transept are two chapels linked together at an angle
of 45 degrees. This arrangement became very popular in the Champagne and in
Flanders, and it was even adopted in Toul, Trier and Xanten.

In the 1170s Abbot Pierre de Celle built a choir ambulatory with radiating chapels
in Saint-Remi in Reims. The chapel in the middle, which has three bays, projects forwards. Wall pillars in the interior form deep window niches, in front of which is a wall
passage leading through the pillars. This wall design was taken up again in the side
aisles of Reims cathedral and in the choir and transept of Auxerre cathedral after
1217, later also in the collegiate church of the Counts of Auxerre, Saint-Martin in
Clamecy (begun 1215), the parish and pilgrimage church of Notre-Dame in Dijon
(1220/1240), in England, and finally in the Liebfrauenkirche in Trier from 1235. The
grouped, lancet-shaped, pointed-arched windows were a characteristic feature of
architecture in the last quarter of the 12th century. The next stage was the double
lancet window with round opening (*oculus*) and foils in the opening, as demonstrated in Chartres between 1194 and 1220 and in the choir of the cathedral of Soissons around 1200.

In around 1180/1190 in the collegiate church of Notre-Dame-en-Vaux in Châlons-
sur-Marne, a choir with three radiating chapels, similar to the choir of Saint-Remi in
Reims, was added to the Romanesque transept of the middle of the 12th century.
As in Reims and Laon the wall elevation is four-tiered: the arcades rest on round
masonry pillars with capitals, the gallery has double arcades under pointed discharging arches and the grouped row triforium connects to the double and triple
lancet windows with narrow mullions. These windows completely break down the
solidity of the blind wall and, together with the large windows in the gallery, bring
a great deal of light into the interior.

Above left, above right and below
Bourges cathedral
Unusually high arcades carry the triforium, arranged in graduated groups, and plate tracery windows (*bottom*). The same articulation is repeated between the two basilical, stepped aisles. Some of the original stained glass is preserved in the windows: the window at the *top left*, created around 1215, shows carpenters at work.

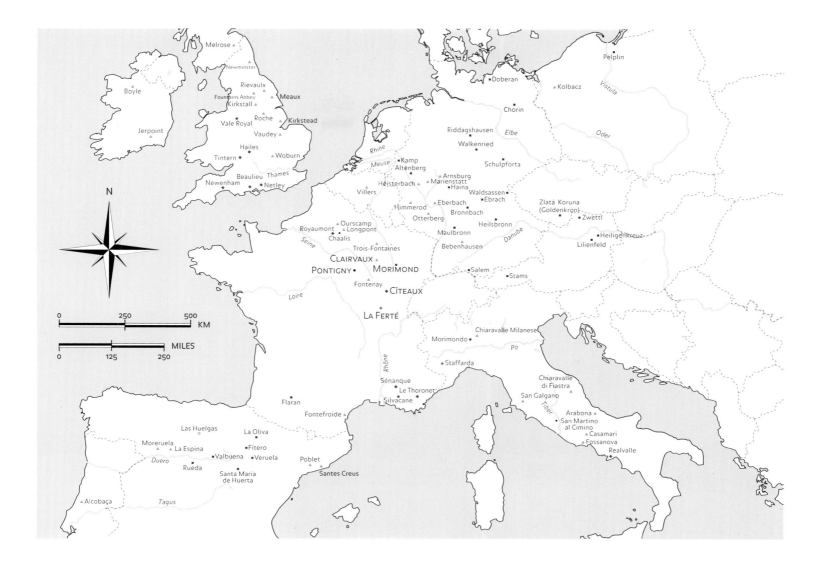

The map shows labels including: Melrose, Newminster, Boyle, Rievaulx, Fountains Abbey, Kirkstall, Meaux, Jerpoint, Vale Royal, Roche, Kirkstead, Vaudey, Hailes, Woburn, Tintern, Netley, Beaulieu, Newenham, Pelplin, Doberan, Kolbacz, Chorin, Riddagshausen, Walkenried, Kamp, Altenberg, Arnsburg, Marienstatt, Haina, Schulpforta, Heisterbach, Villers, Himmerod, Eberbach, Waldsassen, Ebrach, Zlatá Koruna (Goldenkron), Otterberg, Bronnbach, Zwettl, Royaumont, Ourscamp, Longpont, Maulbronn, Heilsbronn, Heiligenkreuz, Chaalis, Bebenhausen, Lilienfeld, Trois-Fontaines, CLAIRVAUX, Salem, PONTIGNY, MORIMOND, Stams, Fontenay, CÎTEAUX, LA FERTÉ, Chiaravalle Milanese, Morimondo, Po, Rhône, Sénanque, Le Thoronet, Silvacane, Staffarda, Chiaravalle di Fiastra, San Galgano, Tiber, Arabona, San Martino al Cimino, Casamari, Fossanova, Realvalle, Flaran, Fontefroide, Las Huelgas, La Oliva, Moreruela, La Espina, Fitero, Valbuena, Veruela, Poblet, Rueda, Santa Maria de Huerta, Santes Creus, Alcobaça, Rhine, Meuse, Thames, Seine, Loire, Elbe, Oder, Vistula, Danube, Duero, Tagus.

Scale: 0 – 250 – 500 KM; 0 – 125 – 250 MILES

Cistercian abbeys in Europe
The map shows the most important Cistercian abbeys founded by around 1300. They all sprang from the original abbeys at Clairvaux (*green*), Cîteaux (*red*), Pontigny (*black*), Morimond (*blue*) and La Ferté (*cross*).

The Influence of the Cistercians

The Cistercian order, founded in Cîteaux in Burgundy in 1098 and confirmed in 1119 by Pope Calixtus II, rose to a position of central significance after 1122 under Bernard of Clairvaux. This order was instrumental in spreading the pointed arch, the cross-rib vault and the bell capital. Cistercian architecture in Burgundy took its influences from older Burgundian building traditions as well as elements of cathedral architecture, in particular those seen in Sens and Langres. These strands, combined with the Cistercian rule of simplicity, led to an independent Burgundian-style Cistercian Gothic, which, by virtue of the order's rigorous organisational structure, quickly spread to Spain, Italy, England, Germany, and, after 1200, well into the East, to Poland, Bohemia and Moravia. The Cistercian monasteries built in these places in turn had an effect on local architecture.

In the new building at Clairvaux, begun after Bernard's death in 1153, the cross-rib vault was introduced into the nave, in place of the pointed tunnel vault. At the same time we find the cross-rib vault in the nave of the monastery church of Pontigny from 1160, where it was also used instead of the groined vault in the side aisles. The wall elevation, however, remained flat and without galleries or triforium. In around 1185 Pontigny took over the idea, seen in the cathedrals, of the choir ambulatory with radiating chapels. When a new choir was built at Cîteaux in around 1190 this was attached square, with rectangular choir ambulatory and chapels; this layout was subsequently popular with the Cistercians and drawn by Villard de Honnecourt as a typical ground plan of a Cistercian church.

The High Gothic and its Emergence in Chartres

The devastating fire on the night of 9/10 June 1194 destroyed the cathedral and a large part of the town of Chartres. Yet France's most precious relic, the *sancta camisia,* the tunic which the Virgin Mary is supposed to have worn when giving birth to her son, and which was brought from Aachen to Chartres by Charles III, remained miraculously undamaged in the crypt. The west portals with their rich figural decoration were also untouched and they were incorporated in the existing west towers (north tower begun in 1134, south tower 1145) when the cathedral was reconstructed.

The new cathedral, more splendid, more beautiful and more richly decorated than its predecessor, was built in 27 years on the foundations of the preserved crypt. Throughout France, especially in the regions under the Capetian kings, the building project captured people's imagination and enthusiasm, and attracted many donations, urged on by sermons, processions to give thanks, and pilgrimages to places where miracles are supposed to have been performed. In just a short time money, materials and labour came together to realise the much admired new cathedral in the little town of Chartres, which had only around 10 000 inhabitants. Building work progressed from east to west. By 1221 the canons were able to take their seats in the choir, the completed vaults already being mentioned in 1220/1221. Between 1220 and 1245 the upper parts of the transept fronts and the two vestibules were constructed.

The nave of Chartres, built by about 1220, has quadripartite cross-rib vaults across rectangular bays, each bay also being associated with a bay in the side aisle. The wall elevation is three-tiered: arcades, row triforium and double lancet windows under a large round window with eight-lobed tracery; these elements completely fill the thin blind wall under the blind ribs. What was new were the proportions of the wall elevation. The windows are as high as the arcades and the dark row triforium

Pages 158 and 159
Cathedral of Notre-Dame, Chartres
In a devastating fire on the night of 10 June 1194 the precious relic of the tunic of the Virgin Mary was miraculously undamaged. This relic had been sent to Aachen by the Byzantine Emperor to Charlemagne, and Charles the Bald donated it to Chartres in 876. Immediately after the fire work began on rebuilding, while preserving the undamaged towers (north tower 1134, south tower begun in 1145), the crypt and the west portal (c. 1150) with its rich sculptural decoration. The choir is described as vaulted in 1220. In around 1210/1220 the large perforated round window was added on the west front. The south transept rose is dated around 1225/1230.

continues as a central band around the entire space. The pillars across and down the nave are alternately round or octagonal and are correspondingly fitted with four octagonal or round vaulting shafts. The capitals of these vaulting shafts are related in size to the cross-section of the shaft. The vaulting shaft supporting the decorative rib in the nave has no capital, and continues through, under the start of the ribs, to the capital of the pillar, interrupted only by an offset impost. On the exterior thick, deep, stepped buttresses and double flying buttresses linked to narrow arcades transfer the loading from the vault. Afterwards, at the same time as the abutment was fitted on the choir, a third flying buttress was added to take wind forces.

Chartres's vault and bay system, three-tier wall elevation, extensive tracery work and rose windows quickly had a wide influence, as seen in the choir of the cathedral of Soissons, which was completed in 1212 and which has a lighter, more advanced system of buttresses than that of Chartres.

Miniature architecture on the royal portal
In the two side portals in the west front of Chartres are figures under small baldachins made up of various architectural forms (here a detail of the front right column of the lefthand side portal). Above this can be seen a part of the decorative band which stretches across all three portals, joining them together as a continuous story of the life of Jesus.

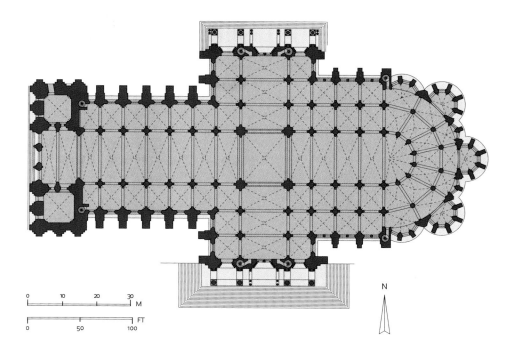

Ground plan of the cathedral of Notre-Dame in Chartres
The ground plan of the cathedral is based around the old crypt, which survived a fire in 1194. The previous church had been built under Bishop Fulbert at the beginning of the 11th century. The crypt stretches under the choir and the aisles; at 108 m in length it is the largest Romanesque crypt in France.

Pythagoras and Priscian
Above the capital frieze of the right reveal of the right-hand portal on the west side of the cathedral of Chartres are figures of Pythagoras and Priscian, embodying arithmetic and grammar, two of the 'Seven Sciences' (*septem artes liberales*) which are personified in the row of figures above (not shown here).

The Development of the Gothic Rose Window

The enormous round window which was built in the west façade of Chartres around 1210/1220 is a combination of perforated or plate tracery, such as that on the north transept of the cathedral of Laon (1180/1190), and a Catherine wheel window made up of a sequence of round arches supported on columns. The window surface, set back behind a profiled, decorated rim, consists of individual slab-like blocks, butted carefully together, out of which the design and the openings have been worked. In the case of the south rose window (about or after 1225), which is a richer progression of the east rose of Laon (1210/1220), and in the north rose window (c. 1230/1240), the regular profiled elements form a grid, leaving virtually no remaining wall surfaces. While on the west façade the three graduated windows of varying widths are separated from the round window by moulding, the five windows under the north rose window are all equal in height, placed close together and extending up

to the rose itself, which is cut into the wall surface on the front. In the case of the younger north rose window the wall spandrels between the row of windows and the circle are also pierced with windows which are separated only by narrow bars. The development of the Gothic tracery rose window is complete.

The Cathedral of Reims

Reims cathedral, the coronation church of the French kings, ranked in national importance alongside the mortuary chapel of Saint-Denis and the palace chapel of the Sainte-Chapelle in Paris. In terms of its architecture and construction it is of great significance both as a whole and for its detail; from the laying of the foundation stone on 12 May 1211 under Archbishop Aubry de Humbert (after the fire of 6 May 1210) and before the uprising of 1233, it was probably the most important, exciting and influential building project in the kingdom. After 1235 further new designs came along such as the final form of the membered column, the pierced tympanum and the sculptural programme. The ground plan, with its long triple-

Walls of stained glass between bundles of vaulting shafts
The view of the crossing, choir and transept of Chartres cathedral gives an impression of the spatial effect in the interior, with its vertical lines, geometric patterns and coloured light. A dark triforium is located above high, broad arcades, and above the triforium are closely spaced lancet windows below a round window with plate tracery. The choir and transept were built and glazed 1194–1220.

aisled nave, transept, choir with ambulatory and radiating chapels and twin-towered façade, was all firmly traditional. However, the elevation and the individual forms such as pillar and tracery, as well as the structural design, were new and highly influential for future developments. The west façade of Reims is of outstanding quality – in the elegance of its composition and in the richness of its ornament, with openwork gablets, tabernacles, tracery and sculptures.

The first master builder was Jean d'Orbais (1211–1231), as shown in a 16th-century drawing by Jacques Cellier of the late 13th-century labyrinth, which was removed from the floor of the central nave in 1778. First he built the choir with ambulatory and radiating chapels. The chapels have the oldest preserved example of real tracery windows. Louis VIII was anointed king here in August 1223, as was Louis IX on 29 November 1226. When the transept and the four east bays of the nave, as far as the vaults, were completed, a dispute between the townspeople and the archbishop halted building work for two years from 1233. During his stay in 1220/1230 Villard de Honnecourt drew a nave bay without vault and buttresses.

Pages 164 and 165
Cathedral of Notre-Dame, Reims
One of the greatest achievements in the development of Gothic cathedrals is the cathedral of Reims, which was built after a fire in 1210 by the master builders Jean d'Orbais, Jean le Loup, Gaucher de Reims, Bernard de Soissons and Robert de Coucy, 1211–1311. The choir and radiating chapels were completed in 1221, and in 1241 the chapter started to use the choir, transept and the four nave bays on the east side. Also dating from this period is the fine buttress system. In around 1285 the graceful rose window was built on the richly articulated west façade, and the towers added by around 1310.

After peace was made between the factions Jean le Loup took over the job of completing the eastern parts, and in 1241 the cathedral chapter was able to start using the choir, which reached as far as the fourth bay in the nave. Following this the rest of the old nave was torn down and, in 1247, Jean le Loup laid the foundations for the west bays of the nave and for the twin-towered westwork. His successor Gaucher de Reims (1247–1255) 'worked on the archivolts and the portals' (*ouvra aux vousseures et portaux*). The master builder Bernard de Soissons (1255–1290) 'made five vaults and worked on the rose window' (*fit cinq voutes et ouvra a l'O*), in other words he completed, around 1285, the nave with the west rose window. Robert de Coucy, who died on 12 November 1311, continued work on the façade – he probably presided over work on the labyrinth.

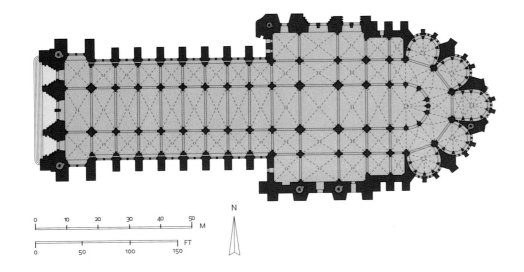

Pages 166 and 167
Cathedral of Reims
The ground plan shows a triple-aisled nave and transept and a choir with ambulatory and radiating chapels.

A tracery attic rises above the choir ambulatory; this view of the interior, looking west, shows the perforated portal tympanum, the pierced triforium and the rose window with tracery extending even into the spandrels.

Pages 168 and 169
Cathedral of Notre-Dame, Amiens
After a devastating fire in 1218 the citizens of Amiens, one of the richest commercial centres in Europe at the time, set about rebuilding their cathedral. Bishop Evrard de Fouilloy laid the foundation stone in 1220. The first section to be completed, around 1230, was the nave, followed in 1243 by the westwork as far as the level of the rose window. The choir and transept were finished by 1264. The rich articulation on the west front is not extended around the towers, which are only slightly deeper, thus creating a main front with three portals, visually merging to create an impression of a continuous base.

The Cathedral of Amiens – The High Point of Gothic Architecture

In 1218 the cathedral in Amiens, one of the richest centres of commerce in France, 150 km north of Paris, fell victim to the flames, like Reims before it. In 1220 Bishop Evrard de Fouilloy began work on a new cathedral, the design influenced by the developments in elevation and ground plan at Reims. However, his master builders, Robert de Luzarches, Thomas Cormont and his son Regnault, also introduced many new ideas, as witnessed by the labyrinth set into the floor of the central nave in 1288. Contrary to tradition, the new building was started not in the east but in the west. When Evrard's successor, Bishop Geoffroy d'Eu, died in 1236 the west façade as far as the gable and the nave had probably been completed, but it is possible that this may not have been the case until 1243. The old church of Saint-Firmin was demolished because it stood in the way of the north transept. The second phase of building was begun with the choir, which by 1247 was so far advanced that Bishop Arnould was buried in the head of the choir ambulatory in that year. The choir

View of the interior of Amiens cathedral
From the west portal of the cathedral (1220–1264) the eye is drawn along a sequence of rectangular cross-rib vaulted bays, past a barely perceptible crossing to the centre of the choir and the perforated end wall.

ground plan follows the same principle as that of Reims, but the Lady chapel in the east projects further than the other chapels. In 1264 the vault was finished. In 1269 Bishop Bernard d'Abbeville had the central choir window put in. The transfer of the relics of Saint Firmin in 1279 indicates that work was completed on the new east sections, and with it, the whole project. The nave of Amiens cathedral, at 133.5 m interior length, is the longest in France, after the now demolished Romanesque monastery church of Cluny.

In the tradition of Viollet-le-Duc Marcel Aubert praised Amiens in 1963: 'Expressed in this building, both in ground plan and elevation, in the proportions of the wall articulation and in the skilled vault construction, there is such a sense of measure, a sureness of taste, a logic and a rhythm of forms, as to make Amiens into one of the most perfect cathedrals of the Middle Ages. It is the epitome of Gothic architecture, its most supreme, classical expression.' Amiens is distinct from Reims in its use of the group triforium which in the choir, built around 1250, is pierced, as in Saint-Denis and the cathedral of Beauvais, and in the way the central bars in the windows are drawn down to the sill of the triforium. This forms an optical link between the window and the triforium and thus the six-panelled tracery window (four-panelled in the choir polygon) is brought together as a single light-filled surface, a tremendous further development of the articulation in the older nave.

If Amiens is regarded as a classic example of Gothic cathedral design, then Reims, Beauvais and the new building of Saint-Denis, begun in 1231, are to be considered innovative, as the creativity and joy of experimentation of their master builders led the way forward to new forms and spatial effects.

Above and below

Cathedral of Amiens

Above the high arcades of the nave and transept a dark triforium stage is inserted, and above that large, light tracery windows. From the ground plan it is clear that the main part of the church is the five-aisled choir with ambulatory and radiating chapels and the triple-aisled transept; the rather short triple-aisled nave and the little-emphasised westwork play a subordinate role. Bu lt 1220–1264.

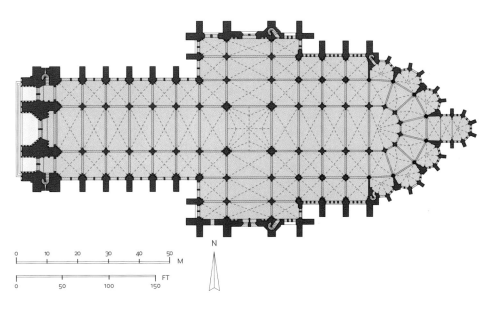

0 10 20 30 40 50 M

0 50 100 150 FT

N

Pages 172 and 173
The royal mortuary church
The abbey church of Saint-Denis near Paris, the resting place of French kings, was rebuilt by Abbot Suger in 1135–1144; in 1231–1241 work was carried out on the choir and transept, and by 1282 also in the nave. The bars in the tracery windows are led down to the sill of the pierced triforium. Above the arcades this gives rise to a single expanse of light, a zone equal in height to the arcade zone. This represents the pinnacle of development in wall articulation and perforation.

The Rebuilding of Saint-Denis

Work on rebuilding the abbey church of Saint-Denis began in 1231, at the same time as work on the choirs of Amiens and Beauvais. The choir, dating from 1140–1144, was rebuilt, except for the choir ambulatory with radiating chapels, as were the transept and the nave as far as the old westwork. In 1241 the choir was in use again, in 1245 the vault was not yet on the monks' choir, that is, the three east bays of the nave. In 1247 records mention the presence in Saint-Denis of Pierre de Montreuil, who was later master builder for the south transept façade in Paris. In 1282 construction work, which amounted practically to a new building, was finished.

The outstanding achievement of the master or masters who worked on Saint-Denis is the complete breaking up of the wall surface. The four-panelled tracery window now filled the entire space between the vaulting shafts and the blind rib, reaching with its mullions over the 'grouped row triforium' (four lancets with double-panel tracery) down to the parapet moulding, thus bringing the pierced triforium (see box in Chapter 'An Interplay of Forces') into a single light space. The transept fronts are also treated accordingly, with the spandrel between the rose circle and the pierced triforium being opened up with tracery, as in the transept of Paris cathedral (1250–1267), and brought together as a single area.

These 'light-walls' are a space-determining element, one which was also used by the second master builder at the cathedral of Troyes, where in the new building, constructed at the beginning of the 13th century, forms from Chartres were adopted. The new master at Troyes, appointed in 1228 and working until 1241, had the same idea, yet his window mullions are even thinner in profile, and the triforium openings more spacious and broader. As a result, they, like the windows, are lighter and more graphic, and in development somewhere between Saint-Denis and Cologne. Just where the pierced triforium emerged as the final development in light enhancement in Gothic cathedrals is unclear. It was used around 1230/1240 in Saint-Denis, Troyes and Saint-Nicaise in Reims (begun in 1231 by the master builder Hugues Libergier), then in the choir of Amiens (c. 1250), in the choir of the small royal foundation church of Saint-Sulpice-de-Favières (begun 1245), in the choir of Beauvais (1227–1272) and finally in Cologne cathedral (1248–1322).

It is presumed that Pierre de Montreuil, master builder for the Sainte-Chapelle in the royal castle of Saint-Germain-en-Laye outside Paris (c. 1238), was influenced by the style of the choir in the cathedral of Amiens and by the Lady chapel there. The tracery in the windows of the Sainte-Chapelle and the west blind rose window correspond to the tracery development in the Île-de-France, and the double-skin wall system is reminiscent of forms in Burgundy and in the Champagne.

Pages 174 and 175
Glass shrine for Christ's Crown of Thorns
King Louis IX, known as Saint Louis, had a double-storey palace chapel built next to his royal palace on the island in the Seine; the chapel was to house a relic, Christ's Crown of Thorns, which the king had acquired in 1239. In 1245 the basic shell of the chapel was complete, and dedication followed n April 1248. The forms are similar to those used in the cathedral of Amiens. The original stained glass, together with the interior paintwork, reconstructed in the 19th century, give a wonderful impression of how this space looked when it was first built, with coloured light streaming into the interior, playing on the floors and bundles of vaulting shafts.

The Sainte-Chapelle – A Glass Shrine

A little later King Louis IX, Saint Louis, had the Sainte-Chapelle erected in his palace on the island in the Seine in Paris. This two-storey construction, built in the tradition of palace chapels, was to house the king's collection of relics, in particular Christ's Crown of Thorns acquired in 1239 from the Byzantine Emperor. Begun in 1241 or a little later, the shell of the building was already complete by 1245, and the chapel consecrated in April 1248.

The chapel consists of a low, hall-like church structure, originally accessible from the courtyard, and above this a high hall space reached from the palace. The walls in the hall space are very finely articulated and have slim, double-panelled tracery windows with stacked trefoils above the lancet windows which are fitted with glowing stained glass telling, in 1134 scenes, the story of the Old and New Testaments and the lives of the saints. In front of the pillars and above a richly arcaded base, gilded and encrusted with glass, mirrored and enamelled tiles, stand larger-than-life-size figures, raised up on brackets and set under baldachins. This feature was seen here for the first time in French architecture in the interior of a building.

The entire interior is decorated in coloured paint, but today it has been extensively restored. The impression is of a precious shrine to hold relics, dominated in the eastern part by a mighty stone baldachin, or tabernacle, raised on a platform. This fitting was added afterwards in 1255 as a place to put the reliquaries; it can be reached via a delicately carved, transparent winding staircase. The Sainte-Chapelle marks the high point of the development of the High Gothic in the Île-de-France. It also represents its technically most useful construction, as evidenced by several

Pages 176 and 177
The Sainte-Chapelle, Paris
Windows in the lower chapel
(1241/1242) of the Sainte-
Chapelle and the finely carved
base of the storey on which the
relics are housed (1255).

iron peripheral tie-beams which are led through the buttresses and windows and at the same time serve as a substitute for the stanchions as bracing for the lead glazing. Together with the deep buttresses they hold the graceful architecture in balance.

This building, too, has links to the Lady chapel in the choir of Amiens, which tends to confirm the 18th-century source stating that Pierre de Montreuil was the master builder on the glass shrine. He rebuilt Saint-Denis (according to a 1247 source), the Lady chapel and the refectory of Saint-Germain-des-Prés in Paris (no longer in existence), perhaps the royal castle chapel of Saint-Germain-en-Laye near Paris and the south transept front of Paris cathedral, the completion of which he took over after the death of Jean de Chelles soon after 1258. Pierre de Montreuil died on 17 March 1267. He seems to have been the most significant and most active master builder in the High Gothic style.

The chapel of Saint-Germain-en-Laye and the Sainte-Chapelle were models for the Lady chapel built in 1259 to the east of the choir of the Benedictine abbey church of Saint-Germer-de-Fly near Beauvais; this church was consecrated before 1267 by Guillaume de Grez, Bishop of Beauvais († 21 February 1267). This Lady chapel also bears the hallmark of Pierre de Montreuil, or at least its design seems to have been influenced by him.

When the west façade of Paris cathedral was finished in 1245 – work that had been started in 1200 under Archbishop Eudes de Sully – the chapels were added on between the prominently projecting buttresses of the nave. In around 1250 the master builder Jean de Chelles erected the new north transept façade, extended by one bay. The many decorative elements are particularly noticeable here – blind galleries, dwarf galleries, openwork gablets, tabernacles, pinnacles, crockets and finials. He began the south façade on 12 February 1258. After de Chelles's death Pierre de Montreuil continued the work, and at the same time started building the choir chapels. The south façade was finished around 1270. The rose window with the pierced spandrels continued the development of the north rose window and represented the high point of tracery roses.

In the case of the west rose window of Paris, created around 1210/1220, the inner 12 trefoil arch arcades surround a circle filled with nosed-cusp 12-lobed tracery; the outer 24 trefoil arch arcades stand alternately on the columns and the arch bosses of the inner row; the spandrel to the jamb of the window is pierced. This window is

A small glass shrine
As in the Sainte-Chapelle in Paris, but smaller and lower, the interior of the Lady chapel of Saint-Germer-de-Fly (dedicated before 1267) has large tracery windows and, at the west end, a graceful rose window. The impression created is that of a light, bright space.

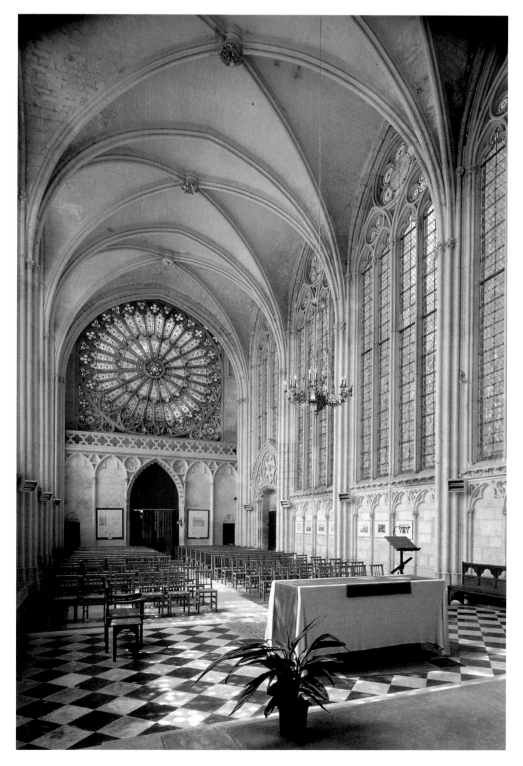

the immediate predecessor to the tracery in the rose built around 1245–1258 by Jean de Chelles on the north transept façade – the latter, divided into 16 parts, has the unusual diameter of 13 m. Lancet rose windows in which the lancets are arranged in two rows are not common. In the spandrel between the outer lancet arches and the jamb of the rose window occur unframed, standing trefoils. The spandrels to the rectangular frame are each filled with framed, standing six-lobed tracery and two smaller, framed, standing quatrefoils; the lower sections are pierced and glazed. The gable was decorated before 1258 with a blind rose, whose central, recumbent six-lobed tracery and trefoils in the surrounding circles were pierced and glazed. The gable design corresponds to the north transept of Saint-Denis of around 1240. The large rose window of Saint-Denis is similar in arrangement to the one in Paris, in the same way that the entire north façade (begun in 1231) of Saint-Denis correspondingly resembles that of Paris. Also to be counted among this group of tracery rose windows is the blind rose on the west wall of the royal castle chapel in Saint-Germain-en-Laye from around 1238.

The west rose of the Lady chapel of the abbey church of Saint-Germer-de-Fly near Beauvais is a continuation of the window rose forms developed on the north transept façades of Saint-Denis and Reims. This form is seen several times in the late 13th century, such as on the west façade of Reims, the west façade of the cathedral of Poitiers and the north transept of the cathedral of Tours.

Saint-Pierre, Beauvais
The choir was begun in 1227, and the ambulatory with radiating chapels completed around 1245. When the triforium, windows and vault were added in 1255–1272, the builders decided to use the pierced triforium tried out previously in Saint-Denis, and to increase still further the height of the interior space while simultaneously reducing the dimensions of the 50-m high buttresses to a minimum. Part of the wide arch span in the centre of the choir collapsed in 1284, and was repaired by 1324. The transept was not built until 1499. Still visible today, to the west of the transept, is the nave of the Early Romanesque church.

Beauvais – The Final Development

When in 1225 the cathedral of Beauvais was the next to fall victim to the flames, Milon de Manteuil started, in 1227, to build a new choir; by around 1245 the choir ambulatory and radiating chapels were ready, and by around 1255 this was followed by the upper floors of the choir, whose vault rose to a height of 48 m. This bold construction was completed in 1272 – supported by high, double buttresses, like slim bars, and thin, double flying buttresses. In 1284, however, part of the vault collapsed in the long choir and had to be rebuilt by halving the arcade widths, introducing sexpartite vaulting and doubling the buttresses again. Rebuilding was finished by 1324. Here, too, as in Amiens, the pierced triforium is integrated into the whole by continuing the central mullion in the window tracery downwards. Beauvais, as a development of the cathedrals in the Île-de-France, overstepped the limits of construction and thus ended that direction. Beauvais itself had no successor; but its forms could be studied in Amiens and Saint-Denis.

The rich development of the Gothic in the Île-de-France quickly spread across all of France during the 13th century, transmitted by the bishops, who had close relations to the king, and who, for the most part, had studied in Paris. These now acquired master builders from the Île-de-France. Thus Jean Deschamps, who knew Beauvais, Cambrai, Amiens, Saint-Denis and Paris, built the cathedral of Clermont-

The pinnacle of delicate articulation and slender proportions
The finely articulated buttress system of the choir of Beauvais cathedral, built 1255–1272, impresses all visitors, and in the Middle Ages, too, it must have been an astonishing sight.

Pages 182 and 183
Soaring heights and wall perforation – the limits of the possible
In the choir of Beauvais cathedral the builders took height develop-ment and perforation of the walls to the very limits of the possible, so much so that in 1284 a part of the choir collapsed. During re-building, carried out until 1324, additional piers were added and the span halved. This created once more sexpartite vaults as in the Early Gothic churches before Chartres.

Ferrand (1248–1265), perhaps also the cathedral of Limoges in 1273, the cathedral of Rodez in 1277 and in 1286 that in Narbonne. He died shortly before 1295 and was laid to rest in the cathedral he built in Clermont.

Many other churches in France also witness to the influence of the Île-de-France: in the Champagne, Saint-Yved in Braine, Orbais-l'Abbaye, the cathedral and Saint-Urbain in Troyes, Saint-Pierre in Bar-sur-Aube, the churches Saint-Quiriace, Saint-Ayoul and Sainte-Croix in Provins, and those in Lagny and Rampillon; in Burgundy the cathedrals of Auxerre, Dijon, Nevers, the choir of the monastery church of Véze-lay, Chablis, Notre-Dame in Dijon, Saint-Thiébault-en-Auxois, Semur-en-Auxois near Dijon and Saint-Martin in Clamecy. Other church buildings inspired by the Île-de-France are Tréguier, Quimper, Saint-Pol-de-Léon, Saint-Brieuc and Dol-de-Bre-tagne in Brittany; Le Mans, Lisieux, Évreux, the choir of Saint-Ouen in Rouen, Coutances, Bayeux and Sées in Normandy, although Coutances and Bayeux only have the two-tier wall elevation and in Coutances, which follows the ground plan of Bourges, there is a richly articulated octagonal crossing tower.

Among the buildings which continued the style of those in the Île-de-France is the excellent example of the church of Saint-Urbain in Troyes, founded in 1261 by

Pope Urban IV on the site of his birthplace. This church adopted the system, found in the Sainte-Chapelle, of iron bands in the choir and transept; at the same time Saint-Urbain cleverly increases the impression of light in the interior by extending the window openings in the pierced triforium, situated below the triple-panelled tracery windows which themselves take up half the height of the space, and leading these window openings down to an unarticulated base in the choir. On the exterior, as in the case of the Sainte-Chapelle and the cathedral of Paris, there are openwork gablets above the windows, linking choir and transept fronts together. The church represents the same level of development as the wall in the high nave of the cathedral of Tours (around 1300).

Finally, also worth mentioning is the small church of Saint-Nazaire in Carcassonne, only 16.8 m high; here the choir and transept were built 1269–1329, by a northern French master builder, presumably on the orders of King Louis IX. The slim columns are further strengthened through the use of iron ties, as also in Amiens and the Sainte-Chapelle. The large tracery rose window in the south transept front is directly reminiscent of the northern French forms found in Saint-Germain-en-Laye, in Saint-Germer-de-Fly and in the Sainte-Chapelle in Paris.

The Late Phase of the Classic Gothic Style

The great importance the mendicant orders in Germany and Italy had for the development of Gothic churches from the middle of the 13th century still has to be
demonstrated in France, due to the lack of building evidence. The only ones that can
be named are the Jacobin church in Toulouse, in which Saint Thomas Aquinas is
buried; it was founded in 1227, and building work started in 1240, but the sections
we see today were not built until after 1260. Narrow, high round pillars separate the
two aisles; slim, triple-panelled tracery windows extend a long way down. During
this time, not only in the churches of the mendicant orders but also in the cathedrals,
grisaille windows began to be used instead of the richly coloured glass windows of
Chartres, Bourges and the Sainte-Chapelle. This, as well as the increase in window
area, led to more light entering the interior, to brighter, clearer spaces. Projects
begun in the third quarter of the 13th century were continued. In around 1300/1310,
however, enthusiasm for building generally waned and, with the start of the Hundred Years' War in 1337 between France and England, it largely came to a halt.

Above and below

Troyes – the ultimate in wall perforation

In the cathedral of Troyes, built by 1241, as in the rebuilding of the abbey church of Saint-Denis (from 1231), the pierced triforium and tracery windows are brought together above the arcades in a single, geometric plane of light, patterned with tracery. Saint-Denis, Beauvais and Troyes represent the pinnacle of achievement in classic Gothic cathedral architecture.

THE GOTHIC STYLE OUTSIDE FRANCE

England, Germany, Spain and Italy

Page 187

The Cologne shrine to the Three Magi
In 1164 Rainald of Dassel, Archbishop of Cologne and Chancellor of Frederick I Barbarossa, brought the bones of the Three Magi to Milan from Cologne. Between 1180 and 1225 Master Nikolaus of Verdun and other master goldsmiths then created for these precious relics an exquisite shrine with rich figural gold work, elaborately decorated with enamelling, repoussé, chasing and filigree work, and adorned with cut and polished precious and semi-precious stones, some dating from antiquity.

Bold measures to prevent a collapse at Wells
In around 1338 scissor arches were built into the crossing arches of Wells cathedral, to prevent the crossing tower from collapsing.

Developments in England

Soon after William the Conqueror, Duke of Normandy, landed in England in 1066, large cathedrals began to be erected in the Norman, that is, northern French, style, starting with Canterbury in 1070. Henry II extended the domain of the Plantagenet Counts of Anjou and became a threat to the French king, for Henry had inherited from his father the county of Anjou, as well as Maine and Touraine. And, by his marriage in 1152 to the divorced wife of the French king Louis VII, Eleanor of Aquitaine, he acquired new territories; he now ruled over more than half of France. But this rule crumbled under his sons Richard the Lionheart and John Lackland. In 1204 Philippe II Auguste conquered Normandy. In addition, Pope Innocent III, the guardian of the next Holy Roman Emperor, the young Frederick II, then growing up in Sicily, succeeded in imposing an interdict on King John of England in 1207.

Until the 14th century French was the language of the English nobility and at court. The Oxford Provisions of 1259 are the first official document written not only in the French or Latin language, but also in English. It stated that royal fiefs might no longer be given to foreigners and that the commanders of the royal fortresses and ports had to be of English extraction. However, French influence remained, as a great number of English students had studied at the University of Paris. In that city there were as many as six English colleges of theology. William of Occam, Robert Grosseteste, Roger Bacon and Duns Scotus all taught there. The universities of Oxford and Cambridge were built on Parisian models.

When Canterbury cathedral burned down in 1174, the monks commissioned William of Sens to rebuild it, and he and his successor, William the Englishman, completed the work in the French Gothic style in 1175–1184. They erected a new choir with ambulatory on the old choir and a round Lady chapel, as well as building a nave, similar in wall articulation to the choir, between the west and east transepts. The three-tier elevation system followed the model of the cathedral of Sens, finished 20 years before. The round pillars with slim colonnettes are reminiscent of Laon, but this form also exists in the Romanesque churches of Normandy and Brittany. The projecting black Purbeck marble colonnettes have similarities with the black slate columns seen in the Romanesque churches in the Rhineland. Parallels to the double transept can be found in France in Romanesque Cluny, and in England this form was used several times, for example in Lincoln, Wells and Salisbury.

From the beginning the French forms which transferred to England were linked with traditional Norman ideas of spatial and wall articulation, and thus the effect was different. Unlike in France, the Early Gothic in England, called the Early English style, felt no striving to unify the spatial design. This difference comes out quite clearly in a comparison of the cathedrals of Reims and Lincoln, where the building structure extends outwards on all sides.

In place of the French twin-towered fronts, English cathedrals show ornamental fronts which have no organic relationship to the nave behind. Bishop Robert Grosseteste had the west façade of Lincoln restyled around 1237/1239. The traditional

Norman vertical articulation from the middle of the 12th century, with three large high niches between wall pillars, was replaced by horizontally layered, decorative blind galleries, in the form of rows of niches running round each level. The screen façade in front of the Romanesque west façade of the cathedral of Peterborough, built 1201–1222/1230, also has a high-pointed arch niche topped by a gable and two smaller niches at the side. A dominant feature of the wall here is the narrow lancet windows, as also seen in the façade of Wells begun in 1229. Lancet windows in groups of three remained a common motif until the middle of the 13th century. Across the front of Wells cathedral, standing in quatrefoil niches, were originally 176 life-size statues, 49 biblical scenes and 30 figures of angels. The façade of Wells had an influence on the design of the west front of Salisbury, built around 1250. The tendency in England towards decoration shows itself in the way façades and tower walls were covered with large and small blind arcades; French Gothic forms were altered again and again as was seen fit, and in the interior, too, linked into the decoration on the wall surfaces.

First seen in Durham and Canterbury, the rib vaulting started in England below the window zone at the height of the capitals of the gallery arcades – this was different from the French cathedrals of the time in Sens and Noyon. The vaults were not, as in France, conceived as a continuation of the vertical lines in the wall, but were suspended in the horizontally articulated wall. By separating the vault it was possible to increase the number of pillar projections and use vaulting shafts in a more decorative way; added to this was the decorative design of the arch jambs and

Pages 190 and 191
Canterbury – the first Gothic construction in England
After a fire in Canterbury cathedral in 1174 which destroyed the choir, the master builder William of Sens began in 1175 to build a new structure, which was completed under William the Englishman by 1184. To the east of the choir and the chapel of the Holy Trinity, a round central structure was erected, the 'Corona', a crypt to hold the bones of Thomas à Becket, murdered in 1170, and the relics of Saint Odo.

Lincoln cathedral
High above the roofs of the houses of Lincoln rises the cathedral, built 1192–1230. On the left the decagonal chapterhouse (finished in 1235/1239) can be seen.

Pages 194 and 195
Lincoln cathedral
The decagonal chapterhouse was
built around 1220. Its vault, constructed later, required a central
column and exterior buttress system (*above*). In 1256 work started
on the Angel Choir (*page 195*).
With its rich wall articulation
(*below*) and large tracery window
opening up the entire flat east
front, this is one of the greatest
Gothic interiors in England.

archivolts both in the triforium and in the window zone. The structural elements of the French cathedrals were devalued and overlaid with ornament. In all areas the English cathedrals lack the feeling of striving for height. And indeed the height of the interior space is generally only half or at most two thirds that found in French cathedrals.

The pillars with slim free-standing columns of Purbeck marble in the seven-bay nave (vaulted before 1233) of the cathedral of Lincoln carry liernes, in addition to the transverse arches and cross ribs which have the same profiling and the same dimensions as the liernes. Also added were further secondary ribs (tiercerons), which start from the same capitals as the cross ribs, but do not extend to the boss, ending instead in pairs in their own keystone on the liernes. This creates a row of stars and bundles of ribs rising up above the capitals, rather like a palm leaf. The bays have hardly any effect in the vaulting. The many ribs give a very wide, longitudinally oriented spatial impression; the characteristic striving for height typical of Gothic cross-rib vaults between transverse arches found in France and Germany is lacking. The area of the vault is independent of the rhythm of the bays in the wall articulation.

The cathedral of Salisbury, begun in 1220, without any links to a predecessor, and completed except for the high crossing tower (14th century) in 1266, is similar to Lincoln and Wells in its proportions; the three-tier wall elevation with double-

The west front of Peterborough cathedral
In 1201–1230 three pointed arches with deep niches were built in front of the Romanesque west façade. On top of each arch is an openwork gable with pinnacle towers. Either side of the façade is a narrow tower.

The west front with 176 statues
The west front of Wells cathedral (1229–1239) was decorated in 1250 with 176 life-size statues, 49 biblical scenes and 30 figures of angels. The figures are placed in quatrefoil niches covering the entire front.

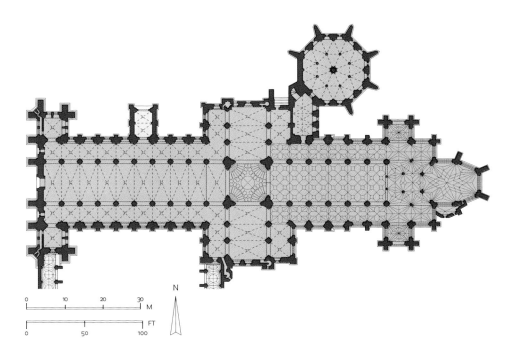

Ground plan of Wells cathedral
The west façade, nave and transept were built in 1180–1239, the chapterhouse around 1290, the east sections 1320–1363 and the Lady chapel in 1326.

Precious jewel
The octagonal chapterhouse on
the north side of the choir at
Wells cathedral was built around
1290. A single central column, an
octagonal pier with eight vaulting
shafts, and eight round piers carry
the rich ribbed vaulting.

skin wall and simple, rather low windows is also related to Lincoln, as is the advent
of the use of coloured marble, seen, too, in Canterbury. The square Lady chapel
behind the retrochoir is a triple-aisled hall space, reminiscent of Saint-Serge in
Angers (Anjou), and its design had a direct influence on the Lady chapel of the cathedral of Winchester.

The Cistercians spread the Gothic style throughout the north of England. In
other areas it was Norman architecture, in particular the double-skin wall, that prepared the ground for the coming of French Gothic influences. In the design of Chichester cathedral, rebuilt after the fire of 1187, the three-tier wall elevation of the
unharmed central nave was taken up, but with pillars with free-standing columns
made of black marble, as in Canterbury. Also worth mentioning are the choir and
transept of the cathedrals of Worcester and Ely, and the south transept of York.

When the abbey church of Westminster in London was rebuilt from 1245, under
Henry III (1216–1272), the French choir ground plan with ambulatory and radiating

Above and below

Salisbury cathedral

In Salisbury cathedral, begun in 1220 and finished in 1266, a clear, symmetrical ground plan combines with an angular perimeter. The wide double-aisled transept separates the linear triple-aisled nave in the west from the ten-bay choir in the east. The choir is further divided at its mid point by a smaller double-aisled transept. This graduation continues throughout both the ground plan and the triple-aisled elevation of arcades, gallery and clerestory windows with wall passage. Salisbury cathedral has a very unified design and is regarded as the best example of the Early English style.

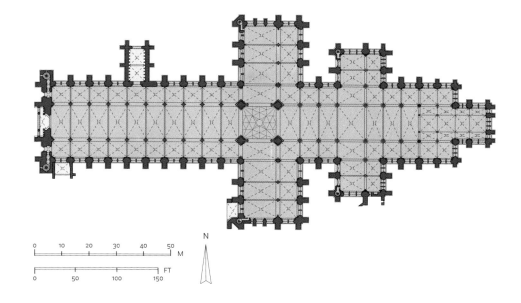

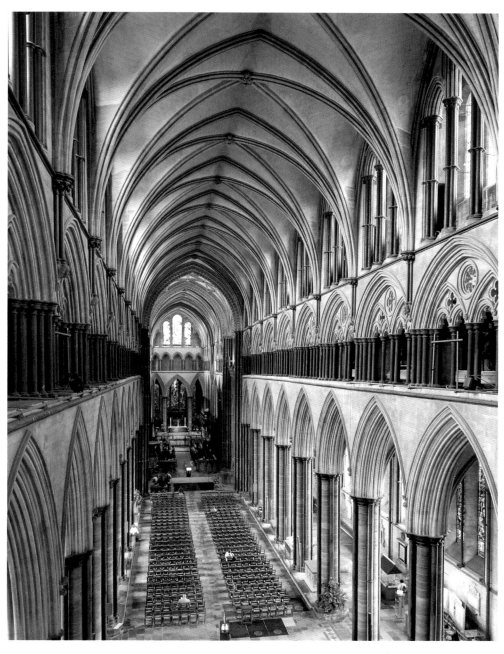

Pages 200 and 201
Built for a king
The choir and transept of Westminster Abbey were rebuilt after
1245 on the orders of Henry III.
The design was strongly influenced by the cathedral of Reims,
and the master builder was Henry
de Reyns, who was in the king's
service.

chapels was introduced. At the same time a new style began, the Decorated style,
which is characterised by ornate tracery windows. Henry de Reyns (possibly from
Reims) is named as the first master builder, and he was followed 1253–1260 by John
de Gloucester and then Robert de Beverly. At 32 m interior height this is the highest of English religious buildings, but is still well below the height of French interiors. The wall elevation of the cathedrals of Reims and Amiens was used for the walls
in the nave, tracery was used in the windows and buttressing for the walls. The unified profiling and size of the transverse and diagonal ribs and the use of the axial rib
conceal the outline of the bays, as in the nave of Lincoln.

Built after the royal abbey church of Westminster were the nave of Lichfield
cathedral, and the triple-aisled, rectangular Angel Choir of Lincoln (1256–c. 1280)

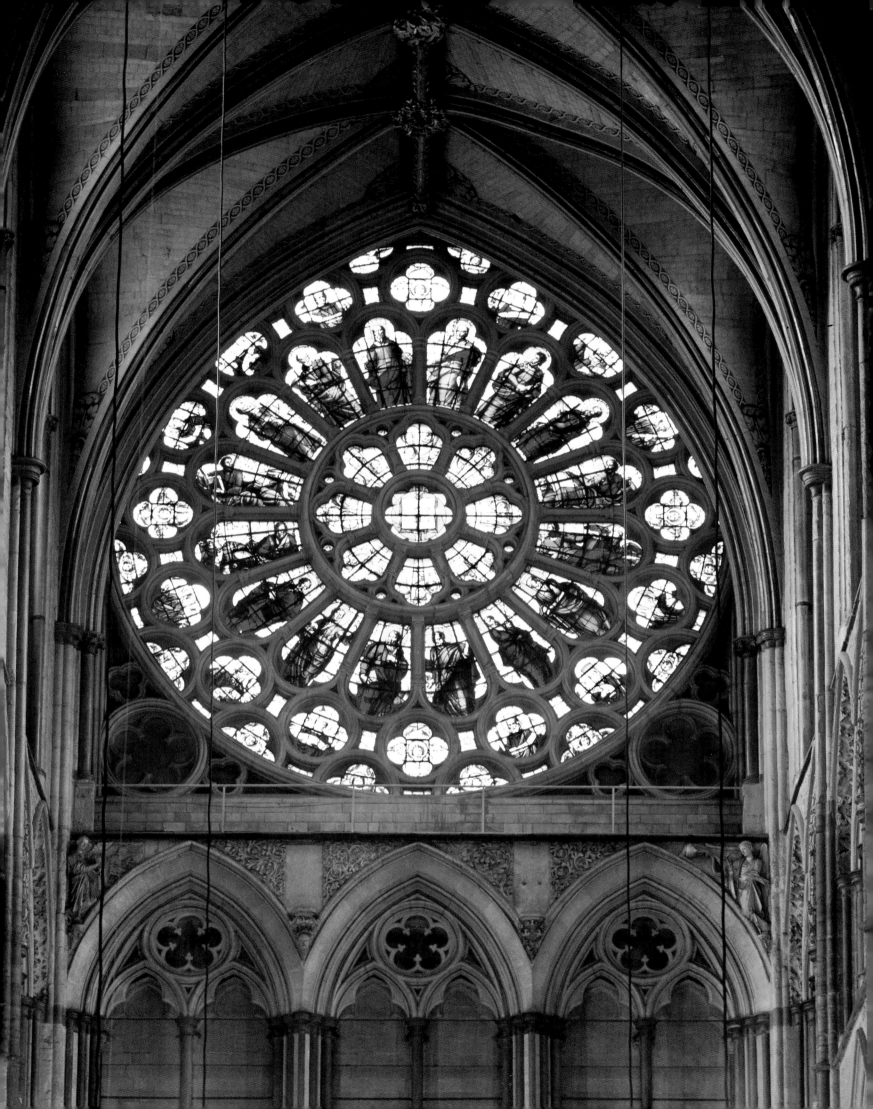

with its rich sculptural wall decoration and large tracery window at the end of the choir. This choir, like the chapterhouse there, was influenced by Westminster Abbey. A number of factors give the Angel Choir its particular richness of design and demonstrate a typically English style of Gothic: the graduation in depth of the archivolts above the double arcades of the triforium and, in front of the clerestory windows, the wall passage opened up with tracery; the 30 figures of angels in the spandrels of the triforium arches and the black Purbeck marble columns contrasting with the light limestone; the bundling together, within shaft rings, of eight vaulting shafts around each pillar, and the finely profiled, much graduated arcade arches and the rib bundles extending from the radiating capitals on the pillars; and finally the narrow profiled rib bundles collected on the corbels, supported by triple vaulting shafts in front of the triforium.

Choir façade of York minster
York's choir façade, planned after 1361 and glazed in 1405, is built in the tradition of other choir façades such as Lincoln (1256–1280), but also has close similarities to the west façade of Winchester, completed in 1366.

North transept of York minster
The north transept and its five slim lancet windows were built around 1234–1251 as an addition to the extravagant new south transept begun in 1227. The royal treasurer John de Romeyn made the funding available for the north transept.

Related to this is the cathedral of Worcester, completed a little earlier, in which the vaults still rest on the encircling moulding of the window sill and are not drawn down as in Lincoln. The east wall is opened in staggered lancet windows, arranged in two levels, similar to the north transept of York minster (1234–1251). While in York in the north transept the vaults, as in Worcester and in the choir of the cathedral of Ely and in Salisbury, begin on the moulding of the window sill, the south transept from 1237 shows the drawn-down start to the vaulting as in the Angel Choir of Lincoln. The richly articulated sculptural design had also been a feature of the minster in Beverley (c. 1220–before 1251) and in the choir of the cathedral of Ely. Salisbury can be mentioned, too, in this context.

The tracery of Westminster Abbey and the choir front in Lincoln, richly decorated with tracery, had extensive influence on further development: namely, on the east window of Ripon cathedral (1288/1290), the Benedictine abbey of St Mary's in York (1270–1294, destroyed), the nave of Lichfield (1257) and the choir of the cathedral of Exeter (c. 1275–1286). Exeter's seven-panel east window, decorated with trefoils and nosed lancet points, was presumably modelled on Old St Paul's in London (c. 1258–1280/1285, destroyed in 1666). The tracery became a key element in the design, such as for example in the nave of York minster, begun in 1292.

During this period a typically English building form, the chapterhouse, a place for the members of the chapter to meet, reached its apogee. These originally circular buildings, such as for example in Worcester around 1125, were built on a polygonal ground plan with tracery window walls. Each one exceeded the next in terms of maximum illumination of its interior. The earliest examples are in Lincoln, finished in 1235, and in Hereford, both of which are, exceptionally, ten-sided. Then followed the octagonal chapterhouses of Westminster Abbey, completed in 1253 (the buttresses in 1377), with four-panelled tracery windows, filled with framed and unframed foil figures (compare Amiens, Saint-Denis, the Sainte-Chapelle), and Salisbury (1263–1284), York (begun in 1290), Southwell (in construction in 1294) and Wells (finished in 1306). The last named extends upwards, like a palm leaf, to a rib vault over a central column. Only in York and Southwell are the chapterhouses without a central support, the vault in Southwell having a wooden roof frame, and spanning an 18-m interior diameter.

In the time after the Crusades, during the 13th century, symmetrically laid-out fortresses started to be built in Britain, such as the ones in Harlech and Beaumaris, in Wales. They differ considerably from the traditional motte and bailey castles, with a mighty keep, such as the Tower of London or Château-Gaillard above Les Andelys, which the English king Richard the Lionheart, also Duke of Normandy, built in 1196/1197 to keep out the French king. This castle stands 100 m high on chalk cliffs on a bend in the Seine about halfway between Rouen and Paris. To modern eyes it is indeed an impregnable fortress, and at that time it controlled movements on the river, with the help of a wooden fort on the opposite bank. But after seven years, in the spring of 1204, the castle was overthrown, through the efforts of sappers who hollowed out the cliffs below it, and by trickery. The soldiers defending the castle had retreated into the impenetrable keep with 5-m thick walls, but they were forced to surrender for lack of supplies. The double rectangular windows under the pointed discharging arches are the only exterior sign of any decoration, yet they characterise this building as Gothic.

The Tower of London
The castle, treasury and state prison of the English king. Built in around 1080 under William I, it was expanded in the 13th century.

Gothic building in brick
The choir of the Marienkirche
in Lübeck was built in 1260–1280
in brick. The ground plan corresponds to the system at Quimper,
which goes back to the cathedral
of Soissons, but those of Tournai
and Cologne also had an influence
on its design. The double-tier
wall elevation has similarities with
those in Coutances and Le Mans.

The Gothic Style in Germany

The territories under German rule in the 12th and 13th centuries, in addition to what is now Germany, were clearly marked: the regions of the Scheldt and Meuse, with Antwerp, Brussels, Maastricht and Liège, the region of Alsace-Lorraine, with Strasbourg and Metz, the eastern parts of Burgundy and the area later to become Switzerland. The areas under Hohenstaufen rule, to the south of the Alps in Upper and Lower Italy, became independent in 1250 and underwent separate architectural development; these are dealt with in the section on Italy.

Unlike in France, Gothic style in Germany did not emerge from a tradition. Instead the Gothic style, which arose in France, was taken over for buildings in Germany, but with very different effects. Individual formal and structural elements were adopted, assimilated and altered as evidenced in tracery work, in the four-tier wall elevation and in buttressing systems, as for example in Bamberg, St Gereon in Cologne, St Georg in Limburg, Magdeburg and Naumburg.

French four-tier wall elevation in Germany
In the construction of Limburg cathedral, started before 1200 and finished in 1225, inspiration came from the French cathedrals such as that of Laon; the individual forms, however, are in the Rhenish Romanesque tradition. A key feature is the four-tier wall elevation of arcades, gallery, triforium and windows, drawn together in a system of bays by the cross-rib vaulting.

In addition, sections of buildings were constructed in the Gothic style, such as the triconch choir (St Elisabeth, Marburg) and the central building (Liebfrauenkirche, Trier). This style was also adopted and further developed in entire buildings, such as in Cologne cathedral and the minster in Strasbourg. During the whole of the 13th century French building sites were important way-stages in the working lives of German stonemasons.

In the beginning German buildings were influenced primarily by Saint-Yved in Braine with its two pairs of chapels, each of them placed diagonally between the choir and the transept, emulated for instance in Trier, Xanten, Oppenheim, Pforzheim and Ahrweiler. Bamberg, Naumburg and Limburg are closely related to Laon (with its four-tier wall elevation, its rich vaulting shaft system and tower formation), Marburg and Trier to Reims and Amiens (with its tracery). The sum total of French developments of the Gothic style was reflected in Cologne cathedral after

St Gereon, Cologne

The decagon of St Gereon was built in 1219–1227, around a Roman oval structure with conches, by a Rhenish master builder familiar with French Gothic cathedrals. He incorporated a Rhenish three-tier wall elevation (conch, gallery, fan window) into the arcades of a two-tier wall elevation (extended, pointed arches on corner vaulting shafts and grouped lancet windows as plate tracery), and combined it with the French Gothic construction (open buttress system) to create a centralised structure with distinct vertical emphasis and great delicacy of spatial effect and articulation.

1248 (based on Amiens, but also Beauvais, Paris and Saint-Denis) and also in the minster in Strasbourg (reminiscent of Saint-Denis). But this style underwent further development in Germany, too, as shown by the clustered pier. These were then 'French' cathedrals, on German soil, but the German examples had little wider influence. What did become evident was the move to close up the wall surfaces, through simple elevations, and a return to the two-tier wall elevation.

The monastic architecture of the Cistercians, with their more ascetic perception of building, paved the way in the 13th century for certain stylistic tendencies in the German Gothic, and left its mark in monasteries such as Altenberg, Arnsburg, Ebrach, Heiligenkreuz, Lilienfeld, Marienstatt and Walkenried. The same trends were observed, too, in the churches of the mendicant orders, who moved away from rich mouldings and diaphanous structures, even sometimes rejecting the vault. This is the case, for example, in the Dominican church in Regensburg and in Erfurt. A hall-

Monumental brick front
Begun in around 1273 and completed before 1319, the west front of the Cistercian abbey church of Chorin is characterised by its building material – brick. The effect created by the brick is that of a towering fortress wall, broken up by the three slim lancet windows with tracery between the unarticulated buttresses, by the blind lancets under the gables of the aisles and by the intricate structures on the top edges of the wall.

type nave was preferred to the basilica. The Marienkirche (1260–1280) and the cathedral (choir from 1266) in Lübeck, with their Gothic forms in brick and echoes of Soissons and Quimper, became influential right across the Baltic regions. The ground plan of the Marienkirche in Lübeck follows that of all the major cathedrals, but shows a distinct tendency to simplification, one not only determined by its material, brick. Very thin vaulting shafts in front of the pillars carry the ribs of the vault.

A particular feature of German Gothic churches is the traditional form of the single and twin-towered westworks, with the towers being raised on square ground plans, as in Freiburg minster, in Marburg, Cologne and Strasbourg. In France, by comparison, for example in Amiens, the west façade had developed without that same spatial depth.

Romanesque architecture in the Rhine-Meuse region, and in Cologne especially, displayed a wide variety of forms that gave depth of space through highly articulated walls and layering. To this was added, in the first third of the 13th century, individual forms and constructions from the French Gothic style. A particularly high-quality example is the decagon, built 1219–1227, in the collegiate church of St Gereon in Cologne; this unique structure was built around an old Roman oval-shaped building with conches. The interior is surrounded by that circle of conches; above are galleries which open in graduated triple arcades with discharging pointed arches. The galleries support, via a cornice, a wall corridor with outer wall pierced by fan windows. This three-tier wall construction, like the gallery churches in the

Cologne's crowning glory
Cologne cathedral, begun in 1248 and not finished until 1880, dominates the skyline on the banks of the Rhine in Cologne. Still today it towers above the roofs of the city.

Rhineland, is made up of pointed arches on corner vaulting shafts rising up from the floor, while the higher main vaulting shafts support the ribs of the vault caps; the ribs end finally in a deep, downward-projecting central boss of leather-covered wood. Above the arcades, in the pointed sections framed by ringed columns, is another wall passage in front of grouped lancet windows with trefoils above.

In the style of the other Cologne buildings, the twin-layered division of the apses and the triconch choirs merges with the vaulted vertical bay formation used in long-naved structures. The master builder fitted a three-tier wall elevation with conch, gallery and fan window into the arcades of the two-floor wall elevation with cross-over pointed arches on corner vaulting shafts and lancet windows. He combined this with a French Gothic construction (buttress system) into a vertically emphasised central space, with great refinement of spatial effect and articulation. The smooth buttresses carry simple flying buttresses which butt to the corner lesenes of the Romanesque articulation of the outer wall. No one building served as a model for this; ideas came instead from many sources: the layering of the walls and the wall passages has parallels with the side aisles of Reims cathedral, and also with Noyon, Rouen and Lausanne; Chartres and Soissons influenced the windows; and the buttress system was modelled on Châlons-sur-Marne and Soissons. Gothic influences can also be seen in the minster in Bonn – in its nave with quintuple arrangement of wall passage arcades in front of the windows, as in the cathedral of Geneva, and in its buttress system.

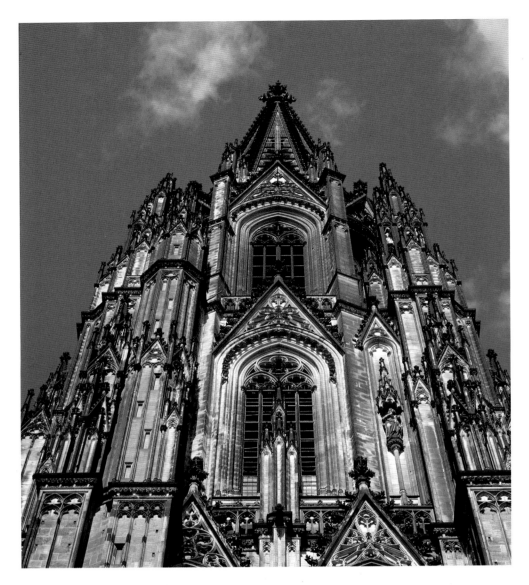

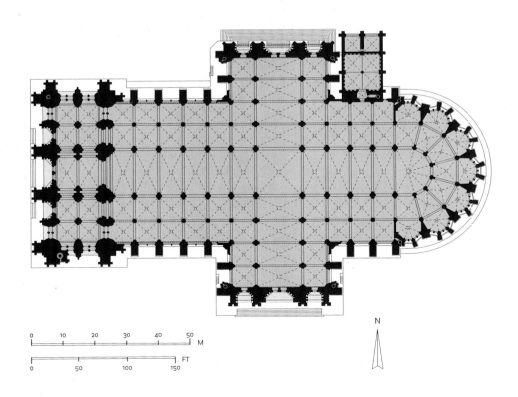

Above left, below left and above right

Cologne cathedral

The master builder of Cologne cathedral, Master Gerhard, modelled the city's cathedral on that of Amiens: the five-aisled arrangement, however, can be traced to the cathedral of Paris. The towers, planned around 1300, but not begun until 50 years later, were not finished until 1880.

0 10 20 30 40 50 M

0 50 100 150 FT

N

Left and right
Gothic walls of light and colour
The choir of Cologne cathedral,
begun in 1248, completed around
1300 and dedicated in 1322,
brought together all the latest
strands of French development
at the time, as achieved in the
cathedrals of Saint-Denis, Amiens
and Beauvais in around 1250. The
high traceried windows are linked
with the tracery of the pierced
triforium.

In St Georg in Limburg/Lahn, begun before 1200, the four-tier wall elevation and the formation of the vaulting shafts are reminiscent of Laon; the two flying buttresses at the choir follow French models, too, but here they have neither a formal nor a structural role. The nave of the cathedral also gives quite a different spatial impression.

The Cistercians brought Burgundian-French ground plans and individual forms to Germany, particularly to south Germany. Ebrach, the west choir and the towers of the cathedral in Bamberg, Maulbronn and the choir of Magdeburg cathedral illustrate clearly the Cistercian influence. Archbishop Albrecht von Magdeburg, who was educated in Paris, started the new building in 1209, its choir with ambulatory and radiating chapels faithfully following the design of French cathedrals. However, in the way these elements are put together there is still a trace of the Late Romanesque sense of form. In the Marienkirche in Gelnhausen, built by 1235/1240, there is a distinct feel of the artistic spatial impression of churches in Lorraine and for example of Notre-Dame in Dijon.

It was not until the construction of St Elisabeth in Marburg (1235–1283) and the Liebfrauenkirche in Trier (1235–1253/1265) that church buildings in Germany began to resemble French Gothic buildings in ground plan and spatial impression, and not just in their adoption of individual Gothic forms such as tracery and pillars (churches in the Champagne region had had an influence here). This is true even though in Marburg the hall church was chosen instead of the basilical form. In Trier cathedral this influence is seen in the use of a centrally-planned structure, cross-shaped and basilical in form, with diagonally placed chapels, in the style of Braine, but with a two-floor elevation. The round pillars with vaulting shafts and membered columns, similar to those in Bourges, carry the crossing arches. There is no open buttressing.

The situation is similar in St Elisabeth, Marburg, in which the tracery windows, as in the chapel choir in Reims, are arranged in two levels one above the other. In Marburg the Teutonic Order of Knights preferred the polygonal triconch choir as a model for the tomb to hold Elisabeth of Thuringia, who was canonised in 1235. It was also their choice for the tombs of the landgraves. The Marburg example had a strong influence on other buildings: on the Minorite church in Cologne (after 1245–1260) and the cathedral in Minden with its long hall-type structure and richly designed, triple-panelled tracery windows (after 1267–1290).

In around the middle of the 13th century French-influenced churches appeared in several places. In the nave of Strasbourg minster the triple wall elevation of Saint-Denis and Troyes was adopted, and the forms of Strasbourg played a role in the design of the nave of Freiburg minster. In 1248 the ground plan of Amiens cathedral was used as a model for Cologne cathedral, and Saint-Denis was taken as a basis for the elevation in Cologne, but using clustered piers, more extended proportions and a delicate grid-shaped triforium of a kind unknown in France. Statues of Christ, Mary and the Apostles were added to the choir piers at half height, as in the Sainte-Chapelle in Paris. In 1259 the builders of the Cistercian monastery church of Altenberg also looked to Amiens and Royaumont, but were more modest in the detail. The buttresses and flying buttresses are smooth and without decoration, and, except for the crossing piers, all the columns are unsectioned round pillars with widely varied foliate capitals in the choir; the wide windows are decorated with rich tracery.

In the rebuilding of Regensburg cathedral after it was hit by fire in 1273, the choir was designed as a simple three-eighths projection; there is no ambulatory with radiating chapels. As in Marburg the choir has two windowed floors, but in between them is a triforium with windows in the outer wall; the wide windows bring ample light into the interior. The choir was completed in 1310, except for the vault. The expansive wall surfaces have vaulting shafts and pointed arches, but there is no feeling here that the architect tried to break up the impression of the wall completely,

Above and below

St Elisabeth, Marburg

This church was begun in 1235 by the Teutonic Order of Knights as a shrine for Saint Elisabeth of Thuringia. Rhenish models were influential in the design of the tri-conch choir, but Reims cathedral and the west half of the nave of Amiens cathedral played a role in the design of the wall articulation, tracery windows and the details.

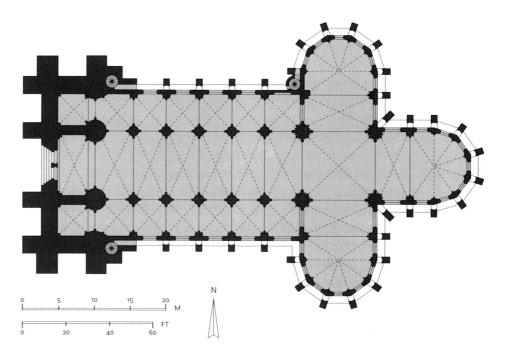

Choir of Magdeburg cathedral
Begun in 1209, the cathedral copies the choir ground plan, with ambulatory and radiating chapels used in French cathedrals, with which Archbishop Albrecht was familiar as a result of his studies in Paris; the choir elevation, however, owes allegiance to the Romanesque tradition of Cistercian architecture (Ebrach, Bamberg, Maulbronn).

as in French cathedrals. The window openings are decorated with tracery, but it is lacking between the vaulting shafts. Bishop Leo der Thundorfer had got to know Gothic cathedral architecture in France, in Dijon and Strasbourg, on his return from the Council of Lyons in 1275, and he had adopted it as his model, but with substantial adaptation.

The mendicant orders, the Dominicans, the Franciscans and others, developed a new regime of life in the 13th century, which was quite distinct in function and organisation from older models. Basing their ideas on an early Christian ideal of poverty and asceticism, which was generally characteristic of these orders, they saw their spiritual welfare work as extending also beyond the existing parish organisation in the towns and focusing on preaching and on the sacrament of penance. The rapid expansion of these orders after the middle of the 13th century led to their churches becoming key features in the towns. The undecorated, simple architecture of these made use of linear-type choirs with polygonal end walls, and large, triple-naved, mostly flat-roofed basilica-type main buildings. The choir of the Dominican church in Regensburg, begun before 1246, and the relatively short choir begun at the same time in the Minorite church in Cologne are examples of the new

Regensburg cathedral

Following a fire in 1273 Regensburg cathedral was rebuilt. The choir was built as a simple three-eighths projection, without ambulatory or radiating chapels. As in Marburg the choir is divided into two window storeys, but with an intermediate pierced triforium. The wide windows bring ample light into the interior. The choir was finished in 1310, except for the vault. Bishop Leo der Thundorfer had become familiar with French cathedrals in 1275, on his journey back from the Council of Lyons. Troyes, in particular, influenced the work on Regensburg, but its forms were strongly adapted.

development, which is expressed in smooth walls with simply articulated arcades and windows cut into the walls.

The west front of Strasbourg minster, started in 1275, marked a high point of the German development of French Gothic architecture. Elevation B gives an impressive picture of the plan originally intended for this masterpiece. Master Erwin († 1319) was the master builder for the lower floors including the rose window. The special nature of this splendid, double-layered wall construction, one which was never surpassed, becomes clear in a comparison with the westwork of the nearby minster of Freiburg, erected from the middle of the 13th century. In around 1280 an octagonal superstructure was added above a low, encircling gallery over the compact lower part; this superstructure, pierced by slim lancet windows with triple-panel tracery, is topped by slim towers, gables and pinnacles, ending finally in a richly pierced pyramidion.

The Influence of the Gothic in Iberian Architecture

Close relations existed between Spain and France after the Moors had been driven
out of Spain with the help of French knights. Catalonia, which was united with Rous-
sillon, was a fiefdom of the French king until 1258. Since 1131 Bernard of Clairvaux
had sent monks to Alfonso VII, King of Castile, and from 1147 he founded several
Cistercian monasteries there: La Espina in the diocese of Palencia, Valbuena and
Santa Maria de Huerta in Castile, the Real Monasterio de Las Huelgas near Burgos,
where the kings of Castile were buried, and finally Poblet.

The influence from the towns in southern France close to Spain was less in the
13th century than that of the big cathedrals in the Île-de-France, because the Spanish clergy had studied at the University of Paris. The cathedral of Ávila, for example,
has a choir and double ambulatory with radiating chapels in the mould of Saint-
Denis, but its elevation has parallels with that of the choir of Vézelay. The cathedral
of Cuenca, begun after 1190, has similarities to Saint-Yved in Braine. The five-aisled
cathedral of Toledo, begun in 1227, is reminiscent of Bourges, because of its non-
projecting transept and the double choir ambulatory; its vault, however, is like
those of Le Mans and Paris, but broader in spatial impression.

The cathedral of Burgos was built along the lines of Bourges between 1221/1222
and 1260, as evident from the ground plan and the triforium, the circle of small
chapels around the choir and the buttressing. However, here, as in Toledo, the
broad arcades, wide windows, heavy columns and lower height give a much altered
spatial effect; in both Toledo and Burgos Mozarabic motifs were used. In the

Pages 216 and 217
Toledo cathedral
In the five-aisled cathedral begun in 1227, much inspiration was
taken from French cathedrals such
as Bourges, Le Mans and Paris. The
proportions of Toledo cathedral
are, however, more compact, and
the height less than that found in
the churches in France.

Pages 218 and 219
The cathedral of León
The distinctive rich tracery of León cathedral, begun in 1255, is strongly influenced by Reims and Amiens. As in Saint-Denis the tracery is associated here, too, with the pierced triforium.

cathdral of León, too, begun around 1255, forms were adopted from Chartres and Reims, such as the ground plan, pillars and foliate capitals, but with the addition of a triforium with outside windows. The cathedral of Burgos influenced Palencia and Lugo in Castile, the cathedral of Osma (from 1236) and Castro Urdiales on the north coast, the abbey church of Rueda in the Ebro valley and San Gil in Burgos. Parish churches tended to take their cue more from the buildings of southern France. Despite the leaning towards French models, the Mozarabic tradition can be found in the tower formations and in the use of rich ornamentation. The rose window in the transept of the cathedral of Évora in Portugal took the form of the French rose window as seen in Chartres and created its own unique style.

The Italian Version of the Gothic

The Gothic style in Italy differs considerably from that seen in the other countries. The typically Gothic articulation of a building was not adopted, nor was the system of buttressing; avoided, too, was the sense of striving to break up the solidity of the walls and the complicated designs for the choir; the forms of the detail are coarser and there are no pinnacles or openwork gablets. The new style first entered the country at the end of the 12th century through the Cistercians, with their monasteries of Fossanova in the Pontine Marshes near Rome and Casamari in Lazio. Further examples are Morimondo in western Lombardy (1182/ 1186–1296), San Galgano near Siena (c. 1224–1288), San Martino al Cimino (1207–after 1257), Santa Maria in Arabona in Abruzzi (from 1208) and Chiaravalle di Fiastra in the Marches (second half of the 12th century), which follows more the simple Burgundian form, and which also had an effect on the building of the cathedral in Siena (from 1250).

Gothic forms from the Île-de-France are to be seen in the church of Sant'Andrea in Vercelli in Piedmont (1219–1224), in its finely articulated cross-rib vault, carried on long vaulting shafts leading down in front of the pillars to the floor; otherwise the wall elevation here is two-tiered, without galleries and triforium, more like the Cistercian churches. This church was built by the much travelled Cardinal Guala Bicchieri, who transmitted what he had seen in Paris and Laon. He brought to this church canons from Saint-Victor near Paris.

Northern French influence in Italy was generally rare, and local building traditions kept their independence. Above all, the twin-towered façade was not found, and the campanile was retained as an unattached part of the building. The spatial form chosen was a broad basilica with widely spaced pillars and walls with

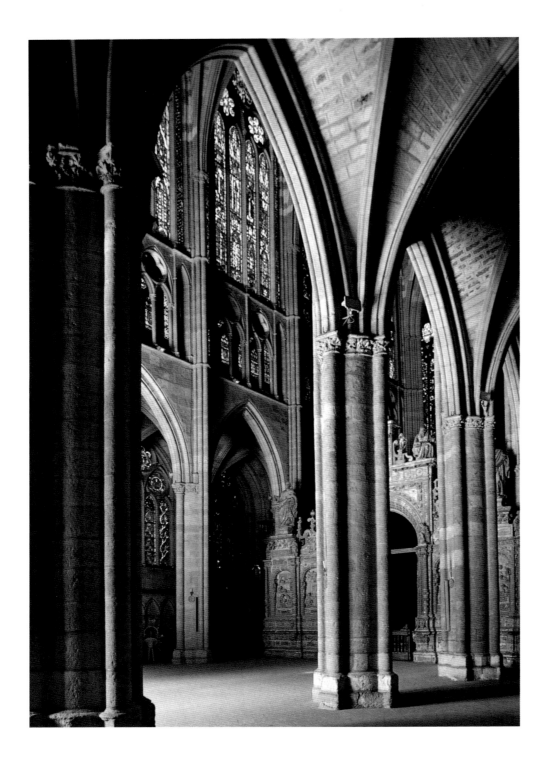

little articulation and few openings. Thus the church of San Francesco in Assisi (1228–1253), in the tradition of palace chapels (the Sainte-Chapelle in Paris), was designed as a two-floor hall church, but with a wider projecting transept and a simple apse. The high walls are decorated with frescoes painted by Giotto, above which is the clerestory with elongated double lancet windows and a wall passage in front.

The preaching rooms erected by the Franciscans were also designed as triple-aisled basilicas: an example is San Francesco in Bologna (1236–1250), a brick-built basilica with choir ambulatory and radiating chapels. The wall is pierced with small windows above the heavy arcades, and above the windows is an old-style sexpartite rib vault. A maturity of development can be seen in the Dominican church of Santa Maria Novella in Florence (1244–1360), where the ground plan with square-ended choir shows Cistercian influence; the triple-aisled nave with high arcades above slim pillars and half-column projections has a unifying spatial effect and the

Santa Maria de Huerta
This Cistercian monastery, founded in 1144, is one of the most important in Spain. The church we see today was started in 1172. The Early Gothic refectory, an elegant Gothic room, is illuminated by four high narrow windows in the gable wall and above them paired windows with six-lobed foils.

cambered vault obviates the need for buttressing – a most perfect and unique creation. The choir of the cathedral of Arezzo (1277–1289) was also constructed without buttressing, but with cambered vaults, and the inner walls and lancet-shaped paired windows with tracery betray a French influence.

In southern Italy, initially under Frederick II of Hohenstaufen, Gothic elements were brought by the Cistercians into an otherwise Islamic-oriented building tradition. Examples are the castles of Frederick II, especially the Castel del Monte (c. 1240), perched on a mountain in Apulia and called the 'Crown of Apulia'; this building is octagonal like an imperial crown or the palatine chapel of Charlemagne in Aachen. Castel del Monte represents a synthesis of Gothic, Roman and Oriental architecture, the Cistercian influence from the Champagne and Burgundy being evident in the wall articulation, cross-rib vaults and capitals. Also worth mentioning are the castles of Trani in Apulia (from 1233), Brindisi (1228–after 1233), Augusta on

Sicily (after 1232), Maniace in Syracuse (after 1232) and the cathedral of Cosenza in Calabria (after 1184–1230).

In 1266 in Rome, Charles of Anjou, brother of Louis IX, was crowned king of the Norman empire's territory in southern Italy. French builders were then attracted to southern Italy, and buildings began to emerge in the style of those of the Île-de-France, western France and Provence. This is shown in the Franciscan church in Messina on Sicily, after 1254, the French-influenced polygonal choir, with ambulatory and radiating chapels but two-tier wall elevation, of San Lorenzo Maggiore in Naples (1270–1285), in San Eligio (from 1270) and San Domenico Maggiore (1289–1324) in Naples. The monasteries built to commemorate the victory of the Hohenstaufen emperor Conradin were erected entirely in the French tradition: Santa Maria della Vittoria in Abruzzi and Santa Maria in Realvalle near Pompeii (1274–1283).

When Hohenstaufen rule came to an end in the towns of Upper Italy, a particular enthusiasm for architecture developed there, expressed in grand palaces with double and triple arcaded windows opening on to the street, decorated with balconies and flights of steps at the entrance. The town halls were also designed in a similar style – buildings like the Palazzo Comunale in Piacenza (after 1280), the Palazzo dei Priori in Perugia (from 1293), and the Palazzo del Podestà in Florence (from 1255). The papal palace in Viterbo in Lazio (1257–1266) also had a loggia, built in 1267, with slim columns and delicate, interlinking arches, betraying a French influence.

All these examples demonstrate the unique way in which the originally French style of the Île-de-France was taken up and adapted in Italy.

Gothic Cistercian church in Italy
The Cistercian abbey church of Fossanova is a splendid demonstration of the simple solidity and stern monumentalism of Cistercian architecture, characterised by Burgundian forms. This is particularly clear in the barrel vault, which has a Romanesque transverse arch but nevertheless in its details bears Gothic forms. The church was begun in around 1186 and dedicated in 1208 by Pope Innocent III.

Above and below

Castel del Monte – the 'Crown of Apulia'

The hunting lodge of Castel del Monte, erected on a mountain in Apulia by Frederick II in around 1240, is a synthesis of Romanesque and Gothic architectural forms filtered through the Cistercian tradition – a singular highpoint in the development of castle architecture.

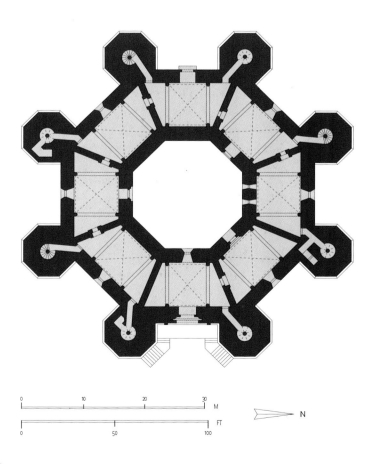

POSTSCRIPT

The Gothic – A Synthesis from Illusion and Rationality

'Weighing the souls'
This section of a stained-glass window at Le Mans cathedral shows a scene from the Last Judgement: the Archangel Michael holds the scales with the sins and the good deeds of one who seeks to enter Heaven. Two devils try to trick the angel out of the soul by weighing down the side of the scales with the sins. This scene is not described in the Bible. It is thought that all the representations of it stem from a sermon by Saint Augustine (354–430): 'The good and the bad deeds will be weighed in a balance ..., and if the number of bad deeds outweighs the good, the soul will be handed over to Hell.

Many factors come together to influence the creation and form of a major building: not only the political and religious position of the person commissioning the work, and the resulting organisation of the building, but also the experience of the person in charge of construction, the master builder. Above all it is the individual forms, their particular shape and the way they are put together that have the most effect on the overall appearance of a building. The forms are the vocabulary, their blending together the grammar of a sentence; together they result in a specific expression.

Since Gothic architecture started to be appreciated, attempts have been made to pick out individual, characteristic forms and pay tribute to their significance in the formal appearance of Gothic cathedrals – forms such as pointed arches, rib vaults, buttressing, openwork gablets and pinnacles, tracery, membered piers and the articulation of the wall. As has been shown, these elements do not represent new inventions, except for tracery, but instead originate in the Romanesque from which they developed.

The Gothic style of architecture in dressed stone emerged primarily in France and developed in the Île-de-France around 1210/1220, in England a little later and in Germany around 1240/1250, with all its technical, structural, architectural and space-forming designs contributing to a formalism, a reduction to repeatable forms and an addition of identical elements in differing dimensions, such as for example the pinnacle and the stone polygonal spire. The interior was then determined by the formal bringing together of nave, transept and choir into a unified space through widely set arcades on slim columns. The Romanesque 'square schematism' and the 'bound system' were overcome through the introduction of rectangular bays, which enabled a larger number of intervals and unlimited serial addition. The pointed arch and the cross-rib vault, which were supported by slim vaulting shafts, spanned the various widths at the same height in space. The choir was no longer raised above a crypt.

The limits of the interior space were marked out by walls which had their own spatial depth, by the triforium and the stained-glass windows between the vaulting shafts in the clerestory. Tracery, geometrically constructed stonework made up of circular arches, was used to throw a grid across the windows, to link in the individual components structurally and to act as an element in the spatial design. Thus a structuring and a linearity of the components emerged, and an extension of flat space by using tracery in a grid-like vertically-oriented system. Everything was subject to a system of geometric order.

What was new was the relationship of tectonic structure and overall appearance, and the special treatment of light, made possible through the introduction of a buttressing system, which together with openwork gablets, pinnacles, finials and crockets opened up the design of the exterior. On the façades the higher sections of the building 'grew', as it were, from behind the lower sections; several layers made up the principle of intersecting tiers or overlapping form. The visual negation

of the structural reality with the loading forces led to an impression of floating and a sense of striving upwards. The visible architecture of the cathedrals is an illusion when one considers the actual technical construction. Geometry and coloured light give an indication of the perfect divine order of the cosmos. The Gothic in the new cathedrals is a masterly harmony of construction, illusion, rationality and theological ideas.

The descriptions of the individual buildings have brought out the stylistic differences between them. The following key words are an attempt to characterise these differences, within the context of French development at the time. The 'individual form' characterises the Early Gothic between 1140 and 1200/1210, the 'compound form' the High Gothic between 1210/1220 and 1270, the 'linear form' the mature Gothic between 1270 and 1370, and the 'pared-down form' the Late Gothic between 1370/1400 and 1520. As has been shown, these phases occur at different times in England, Germany, Spain and Italy, and there are regional differences. The term 'Gothic' is only seemingly a clear definition of a style, but it falls short of conveying the true splendour of the wonderful buildings it is used to describe.

'The measured work' – geometry

The double-layered tracery rose in the west front of Strasbourg minster is a stone embodiment of a Gothic idea: the *ordo*, or world order, is represented in geometry, and this order is created and directed by the world's master builder.

Page 227

Skeleton and glass

The north transept and choir of the abbey church of Saint-Denis near Paris, where the French kings were buried, was transformed in 1231–1241 into a masterpiece of vertical articulation and stained glass.

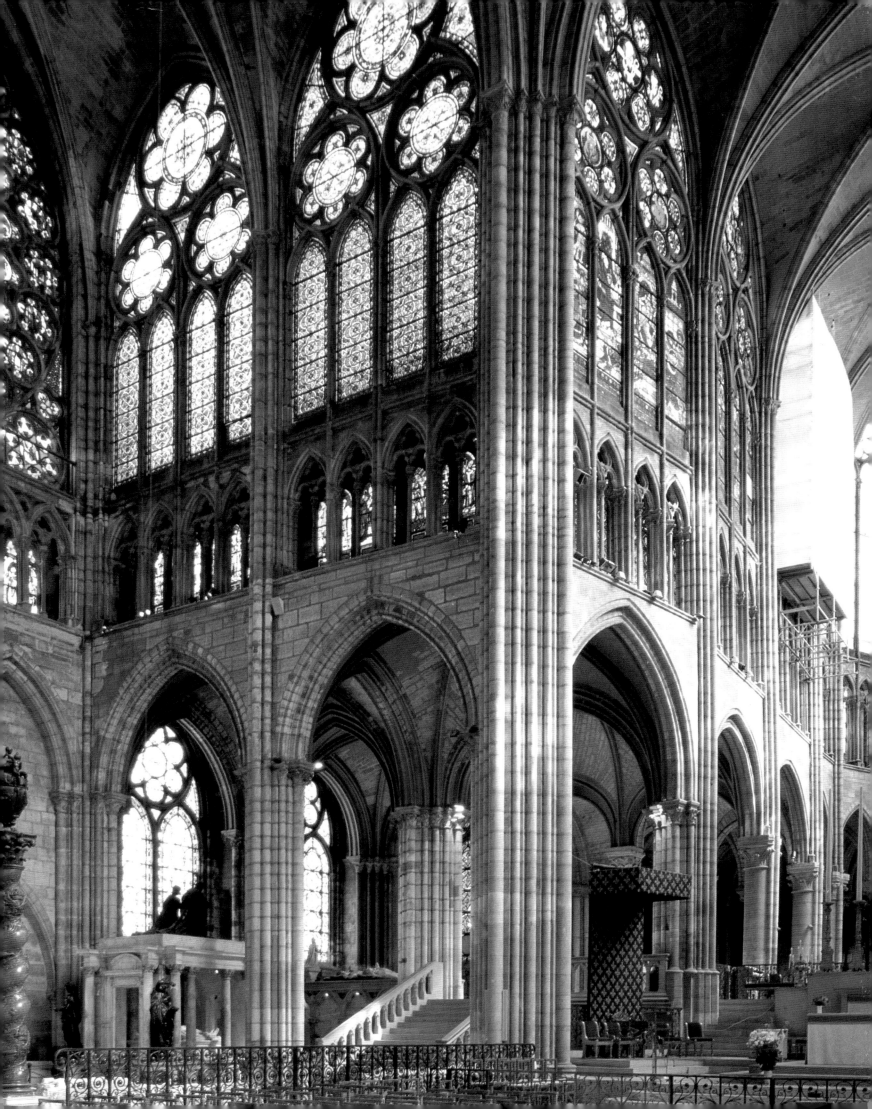

CHRONOLOGICAL TABLE

Monuments

1130–1144 Saint-Denis: westwork and choir
1132–1145 Saint-Germer-de-Fly: choir of the abbey church
1140–1168 Sens: cathedral
1151–1191 Senlis: cathedral
1160–1170 Noyon: transept of the cathedral
1160–1205 Laon: cathedral
1163–1196 Paris: cathedral
1165–1200 Reims: choir of Saint-Remi
1170–1217 Châlons-sur-Marne: Notre-Dame-en-Vaux
from 1176 Soissons: south transept of the cathedral
1194–1220 Chartres: cathedral
1195–1208 Braine: Saint-Yved
1195–1214 Bourges: choir of the cathedral
1196–1197 Château-Gaillard
1196–1220 Paris: westwork of the cathedral
1200–1212 Soissons: choir and eastern nave bays of the cathedral
1205–1215 Laon: choir of the cathedral

1175–1184 Canterbury: choir and Trinity Chapel of the cathedral
c. 1180 St David's (Wales): start of the cathedral
1180–1239 Wells: cathedral
1192–1230 Lincoln: choir of the cathedral

1130–1210	France 1130–1210	England 1130–1210

Events

West façade of the cathedral Notre-Dame, Paris

1137–1180 King Louis VII
1147 Louis VII leads the French crusaders
1152 The whole of the west of France comes under English rule through the marriage of Eleanor of Aquitaine to the Plantagenet heir, later King Henry II
1153 Bernard of Clairvaux dies
1157 Parliament in Besançon: power struggle between the Emperor and the Pope
1160 Pope Alexander III goes to France
1176 Beginning of the Albigensian (Waldensian) movement in southern France
1180–1223 King Philippe II Auguste
1187 Alliance between Philippe II Auguste of France and Frederick I, Barbarossa against the Angevins and the Guelphs
1202–1204 Philippe II Auguste conquers the English-held regions in France, except for Guyenne
1209–1229 Albigensian wars

1154–1189 Henry II of England, first Plantagenet king; House of Anjou-Plantagenet
1164 Constitution of Clarendon
1169 Henry the Lion, Duke of Saxony, marries Mathilda of England
1170 Murder of Thomas à Becket
1189–1199 King Richard I, the Lionheart
1192 Richard the Lionheart and Saladin agree an armistice
1193 Richard the Lionheart is held captive in Austria on his return from the third Crusade
1199–1216 King John

Western part of the abbey church
of Saint-Denis near Paris

South transept of Soissons
cathedral

1171–1181 Worms: west choir of the cathedral
1200–1207 Ebrach: St Michael's Chapel of the
Cistercian monastery
1200–1235 Limburg: cathedral St Georg
1209–1232 Magdeburg: choir of the cathedral

1182–1296 Morimondo: Cistercian monastery
church
1184–1230 Cosenza (Calabria): cathedral
1187–1208 Fossanova: Cistercian monastery
church
1190–1250 Cuenca: cathedral
1203–1217 Casamari: Cistercian monastery
church

Germany
1130–1165

Germany
1165–1210

Italy/Spain
1130–1210

1125–1137 Emperor Lothar III (Duke of Saxony)
1132–1133 First Italian campaign of Lothar III;
coronation as Holy Roman Emperor
in the Lateran by Pope Innocent
1136/1137 Second Italian campaign by Lothar
III; Norman territories in Lower Italy
conquered
1138–1139 Battle between the Hohenstaufen
supporters (Ghibellines) and the
Guelphs
1138–1152 King Conrad III Hohenstaufen
1139–1180 Henry the Lion recognised by all as
Duke of Saxony
1147–1149 Second Crusade; Conrad III leads
the German crusaders
1152–1190 Emperor Frederick I, Barbarossa
1154 Henry the Lion becomes Duke of
Bavaria
1154–1155 First Italian campaign of Frederick I
1156 Frederick I marries Beatrice, the
heiress to the throne of Burgundy
(Franche-Comté)
1165 The Würzburg Oath: agreements
between Frederick I and Henry II of
England against Pope Alexander III

1165 Emperor Charlemagne beatified
1169 Henry the Lion marries Mathilda of
England; Frederick I allows his son,
Henry VI, to be elected king
1178–1180 Trial of Henry the Lion; Henry loses
his fiefs and is deposed
1190 Frederick I is victorious at Iconium
against the Turks and drowns on
10.06.1190 in the Saleph
1190–1197 Emperor Henry VI
1198 The struggle for the imperial throne
between the Ghibellines and the
Guelphs
1202–1204 Fourth Crusade; the crusaders
conquer Constantinople
1209 Otto IV is crowned Emperor in
Rome

1139 Pope Innocent II places the
crusaders under the protection of
the Church
1145–1153 Pope Eugene III
1146 Alliance between the Pope, Conrad
III and Manuel against Roger of
Sicily; Alfonso VII of Castile fights
against the Moors; Córdoba is taken
1154 The University of Bologna is
founded, as the first university in
the Latin West
1154–1159 Pope Hadrian IV
1158–1214 Alfonso VIII of Castile
1159–1181 Pope Alexander III
1159–1164 Victor IV, Antipope appointed by
the Emperor
1160 Council of Pavia recognises Pope
Victor IV; Pope Alexander III goes to
France
1177 Peace of Venice: Frederick I
reconciled with Pope Alexander III
1187 Saladin victorious over the
Christians at Hittin on Lake Galilee;
conquers Jerusalem
1198–1216 Innocent III: high point of Papal
power

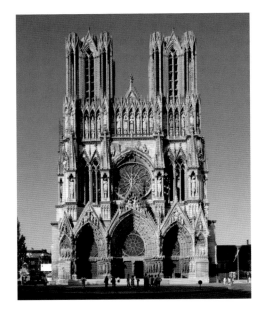

West façade of Reims cathedral

Monuments

1211–1241	Reims: cathedral
1217–1230	Auxerre: choir of the cathedral
1220	Amiens: foundation stone of the cathedral laid
1220–1240	Dijon: Notre-Dame
1220–1250	Coutances: cathedral
1227–1272	Beauvais: choir of the cathedral
1231–1282	Saint-Denis: rebuilding
before 1233	Tours: cathedral
c. 1238	Saint-Germain-en-Laye, near Paris: royal castle chapel
before 1241	Troyes: choir of the cathedral
1241–1248	Paris: Sainte-Chapelle
1248–1280	Clermont-Ferrand: cathedral
1250–1267	Paris: transept fronts of the cathedral
1255–1285	Reims: westwork of the cathedral
1259–1267	Saint-Germer-de-Fly: Lady chapel
1262–1275	Troyes: Saint-Urbain

1220–1251	Beverley: minster
1220–1266	Salisbury: cathedral
1224–1232	Worcester: choir of the cathedral
1229–1239	Wells: west façade of the cathedral
1234–1251	York: transept of the minster
1234–1252	Ely: choir of the cathedral
1237/1239	Lincoln: chapterhouse
c. 1240	Lincoln: start of west façade of the cathedral
1245–1272	London: Westminster Abbey
c. 1250	Salisbury: west façade
1256–1280	Lincoln: Angel Choir of the cathedral
1257	Lichfield: start of nave
1263–1284	Salisbury: chapterhouse
1275–1286	Exeter: choir of the cathedral
1292	York: start of nave of the minster

1210–1300	France 1210–1300	England 1210–1300

Events

1223–1226	King Louis VIII
1226–1270	King Louis IX, the Saint
1270–1285	King Philippe III, the Bold; conquering of Provence and the County of Toulouse
1285–1314	King Philippe IV, the Fair; France at the pinnacle of its power in the medieval period

1214	Philippe II Auguste victorious at Bouvines over the English allied with the Emperor Otto IV
1215	Magna Carta Libertatum: uprising of the nobility forces King John to introduce legal protection against royal despotism
1216–1272	King Henry III
1258–1265	Rising of the barons
1272–1307	King Edward I

Triple-aisled Angel Choir of Lincoln cathedral

Nave of Canterbury
cathedral

1219–1227 Cologne: decagon of St Gereon
1225–1237 Bamberg: west choir
1235–1265 Trier: Liebfrauenkirche
1235–1283 Marburg: St Elisabeth
1240–1275 Strasbourg: nave of the minster
1246–1270 Regensburg: choir of the Dominican
church
1248–1322 Cologne: choir of the cathedral
c. 1250 Naumburg: west choir
1259–1276 Altenberg: choir of the Cistercian
church

1260–1280 Lübeck: choir of the Marienkirche
1267–1290 Minden: hall nave of the cathedral
1273–1310 Regensburg: choir
1273–1319 Chorin: Cistercian church
1275–1365 Strasbourg: westwork
c. 1280 Freiburg: start of the octagon of the
minster tower
1288–1295 Heiligenkreuz: choir of the
Cistercian church

1219–1224 Vercelli: Sant´Andrea
1221–1260 Burgos: cathedral
1227 Toledo: start of the cathedral
1228–1253 Assisi: San Francesco
1236–1250 Bologna: San Francesco
c. 1240 Castel del Monte (Apulia)
1244–1360 Florence: Santa Maria Novella
1250 Siena: start of the cathedral
1254 Messina: start of the Franciscan
church
1255 Florence: start of the Palazzo del
Podestà
c. 1255 León: start of the cathedral
1257–1266 Viterbo: papal palace
1270–1285 Naples: San Lorenzo Maggiore
1277–1289 Arezzo: cathedral
after 1280 Piacenza: Palazzo Comunale

Germany
1210–1260

Germany
1260–1300

Italy/Spain
1210–1300

1212–1250 Frederick II, King of Sicily, German
King and Holy Roman Emperor
1213 Golden Bull of Eger: renewal, under
Frederick II, of concessions made by
the Pope
1220 Pope Honorius III crowns
Frederick II Emperor
1228–1229 Fifth Crusade
1248–1254 Sixth Crusade
1250–1254 King Conrad IV
1256–1273 Interregnum

1273–1291 King Rudolf von Habsburg;
Germany breaks up into territorial
principalities
1292–1298 King Adolf von Nassau
1298–1308 King Albrecht I von Habsburg

1215 Lateran Synod: Fourth Lateran
Council resolves on persecution of
heretics in the Inquisition
1225 Guelphs and Ghibellines fight for
control of the Upper Italian cities;
Frederick II founds the University of
Naples
1266–1285 Charles of Anjou rules southern Italy
from Naples

West façade of Strasbourg
minster

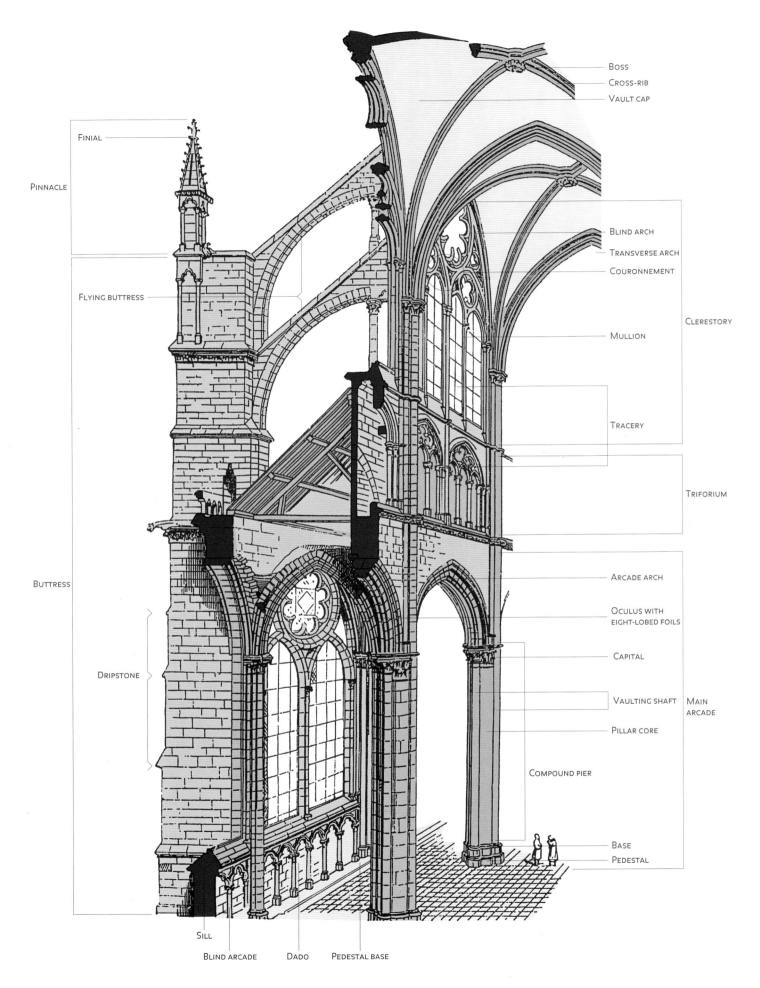

BOSS

CROSS-RIB

VAULT CAP

FINIAL

PINNACLE

BLIND ARCH

TRANSVERSE ARCH

COURONNEMENT

FLYING BUTTRESS

CLERESTORY

MULLION

TRACERY

TRIFORIUM

BUTTRESS

ARCADE ARCH

OCULUS WITH
EIGHT-LOBED FOILS

DRIPSTONE

CAPITAL

VAULTING SHAFT

MAIN
ARCADE

PILLAR CORE

COMPOUND PIER

BASE

PEDESTAL

SILL

BLIND ARCADE   DADO   PEDESTAL BASE

Glossary

Abacus: Slab, uppermost member of the → capital of a → column.

Abutment system: → Buttress system.

Aisle: The space flanking and parallel to the → nave; separated from the nave by → arcades.

Ambulatory: A spatial zone, lower than and encircling the central part of the choir, often a continuation of the side → aisles.

Angulated: Continuing a horizontal wall articulation (→ cornice, entablature) around a projecting vertical member (→ pilaster, → shaft).

Apse: A semicircular, vaulted → choir.

Arcade, arcading: An arch or a line of arches, raised on → pillars or → columns.

Arched buttress: → Flying buttress.

Archivolt: Profiled or decorated arch.

Baldachin: An ornamental canopy over cult objects; also a projecting, mostly polygonal stone cover over statuettes, supported on corbels.

Bar: → Mullion.

Barrel vault, tunnel vault: Simple → vault of semicircular section with no cross-vaults.

Base: The projecting, profiled bottom part of a → column or → pier.

Basilica: A church with three aisles (sometimes five) with a central → aisle raised by → clerestory windows.

Bay span: Spatial arrangement of a vaulted → basilica in which each square bay in the central section of the nave is associated with two square bays of half length in the side aisles.

Blind arcade: Blind arch, window, tracery etc. A feature applied to a wall surface or standing in front of it.

Boss: Stone at the apex of an arch; in the case of rib → vaults it is the main intersection of the → ribs at the apex of the vault; keystone.

Bundle pier: A pier or pillar to which is attached all around three-quarter columns of larger and smaller diameters, called → vaulting shafts.

Buttress: On the outside of a building, a projecting or free-standing pillar in the exterior wall of a church which takes up the lateral thrust from the vaults; in the case of a → basilica the buttresses rise up above the lower → eaves of the aisle and take the thrust from the → flying buttresses; → buttress system.

Buttress system: The construction system composed of → buttresses and → flying buttresses which directs the shear and compression loads from a → cross-rib vault and the wind pressure from the → clerestory wall.

Camber, cambered vault: Convex curvature of the rising → vault cell in the case of a cross vault.

Capital: Projecting head piece of a column, consisting of → abacus, main section and necking.

Cathedral: Bishop's church with the cathedra, or bishop's chair.

Chapterhouse: Meeting room in a monastery, cathedral or collegiate church; place where the rules of the chapter, order or monastery are read out.

Choir: The part of the church where the choir sings and the priests pray; mostly at the east end of the church.

Choir bay, antechoir: Area between the start of the choir and the rounded or perforated end wall of the choir.

Choir polygon: Many-sided, open → apse as opposed to usual semicircular form.

Clerestory: The windowed part of a → basilica above the side → aisles and above the wall of the central part of the nave.

Column: A supporting member with circular, polygonal or profiled plan, consisting of a → base, → shaft and → capital.

Compound pier: → Membered pier.

Conch: Half-round area with semi-dome, → apse.

Cornice: Generally a horizontal element which divides a wall into different sections.

Couronnement: An arch bay, filled with → tracery, in a window.

Crocket: Cross-shaped stylised leaves decorating a central shaft; used to crown → pinnacles etc.

Crossing: The space where the → transept crosses the main axis of a church.

Cross-rib vault: → Groined vault with groins underpinned by → ribs which cross in the middle of the bay.

Crypt: Low room under the → choir of a church, used for funerary or reliquary cults.

Cupola, dome: Spherical → vault, mostly in the shape of a spherical segment above a circular ground plan; the most common form of a cupola is the hemisphere.

Decagon: Ten-sided space.

Dwarf gallery: A low passage below the → eaves, screened by a small arcade.

En délit: Shafts on engaged columns and longer vaulting shafts which stand in front of the pier and are not worked from the same stone blocks.

Finial: Ornament at the point of a → pinnacle or gable etc.

Flying buttress: On the outside of a building, an arch rising at an angle, to take up the vault thrust from the → clerestory wall of the → nave of a → basilica and direct it above the → aisles into the → buttresses.

Foil: Circular segment which is put together concentrically with other foils to form → tracery figures.

Framed square moulding: A common form of moulding used in the High and Late Romanesque period in the Rhineland. Consists of rows of square shapes.

Gallery: Covered corridor often with richly decorated columns on the open side; → dwarf gallery.

Gallery of Kings: Sequence of statues under → arcades, in niches and under → baldachins on the façade of Gothic cathedrals.

Gargoyle: A waterspout projecting from the roof gutter of a building, often carved into a grotesque figure.

Groined vault: Form created by two intersecting → barrel vaults of the same height; consists of four triangular intersecting → vault cells which meet in groins in the centre of the bay.

Hall church: A church with one undivided space; a church with several aisles all of the same height.

Hood-mould, dripstone: → Cornice with sloping ridge undercut by a deep valley.

Horizontal flying buttress: A horizontal arch taking the shear forces between two uprights; → flying buttress.

Impost: Profiled slab above a capital of a column or pillar from which springs an arch or → vault.

Jamb, ingoing: Sloping reveal of a portal or window, often graduated or divided into sections by profiles; sometimes containing statuettes.

Lancet arch: Slim, exaggeratedly pointed arch with low span.

Lesene: Shallow vertical projection on a wall; rarely has a → base and small → impost, often linked with blind arch or arch frieze.

Lierne rib: A secondary rib in the fan or net vault, which springs either from an → impost or from a central → boss.

Long choir: A form of choir developed by the mendicant orders; a particularly long → choir bay in front of the choir polygon.

Membered pier, pillar: Round pier or pillar with four three-quarter column projections, resting on a joint base and with foliated capital; the preliminary stage towards the → bundle pier; membered column.

Minster: (Latin *monasterium*) The monastery-like community of members of a cathedral chapter and canons; → cathedral.

Mullion: A vertical post or other upright dividing a window or other opening into two or more lights; main bar; secondary bar.

Nave: The middle aisle or multiple-aisled main part of a church, between the → westwork and → crossing or → choir, divided by arcades from the side → aisles.

Nave arch: Arch separating equal height → aisles in a → hall church.

Openwork gablet: Gable-shaped motif above Gothic portals and windows, often finished with → tracery decoration, → crockets, → pinnacles and finials.

Pier: Masonry support between openings (arcades, doors, windows etc.) with rectangular, square or polygonal cross-section, also round (but does not taper and has no → capital, as with a column). The pier can have a → base, but must have an → impost (otherwise it is just part of the wall).

Pilaster: Wall pier with → base and → capital.

Pillar: A masonry support, the → shaft of which consists of rectangular, octagonal, circular or cruciform blocks; it does not taper, has an → impost, and, unlike a → column, need not be cylindrical.

Pinnacle: Narrow, pointed tower on → buttresses and → openwork gablets or on portals and → galleries; perched on top of the main section crowned with small gables is the → pyramidion.

Plinth: Square slab on which stands the → base of a column, pilaster or door frame.

Polygon: Shape with many sides.

Pyramidion: A pointed, pyramid-shaped cap, decorated with → finials and → crockets, on top of a → pinnacle.

Radiating chapels: The sequence of chapels arranged around the choir → ambulatory.

Retrochoir: In English churches an → ambulatory behind the choir of a church. Corresponds to the side aisles of the → nave.

Rib: A curved moulding projecting from the underside of a masonry → vault. Can be combined to form a wide range of rib patterns.

Ridge: The apex of a roof.

Rose window: A round window filled with → tracery.

Shaft: The trunk of a column or pillar; a slender column attached to a support.

Sill: A horizontal bottom member of a window; tilted forwards and projecting outwards from the wall below.

Stilting, stilted: Raising an arch or → vault by lengthening the vertical section above the → impost before the start of the curve.

Tabernacle: On the outside of a building: → pinnacle-like but open construction with a corner pillar and pointed roof, often containing statues.

Tierceron: A secondary rib springing from an → impost in a fan or net vault.

Tracery: Geometrically constructed building ornament to divide the arch bay (→ couronnement) above the impost line from windows; later also to articulate wall surfaces (against a wall or free-standing) and for parapets. The basic forms used are the → foil and the triskele, often used in groups (trefoil, quatrefoil etc.). Below the impost line the tracery continues as → mullions.

Transept: A → nave at right-angles to the main axis of the church. A transept may be divided into areas of different height.

Transverse arch: An arch whose span is crosswise to the longitudinal axis of a → vault; it separates the individual bays of the vault.

Trefoil choir: → Triconch choir.

Tribune gallery: Space above the side → aisles or choir → ambulatories, spanning the central → nave in the west, and open to the nave by → arcades.

Triconch choir, trefoil choir: Choir laid out in trefoil-shaped → conches; triple-conch choir.

Triforium: A passage in the wall between the → arcades or the → gallery and the window zone of a → basilica, at the height of the roofs above the aisles. A blind triforium has no passageway, and blind arches are placed in front of the wall; a false triforium has arcades or similar which open to the roof; a pierced triforium has windows in the outer wall of the passage.

Trumeau: The central stone pillar of a two-leaved portal.

Tympanum: A triangular or segmental space above the lintel of a portal.

Vault: A curved wall surface covering a space; self-supporting and resting on abutments; in Gothic architecture mostly divided by groins or → ribs into several → vault cells.

Vault bay: An area of vaulting limited by two transverse ribs.

Vault cap, cell: An area of the vault marked out by groins or → ribs.

Vault, sexpartite: → Cross-rib vault which has an added transversal → rib in the centre of the bay.

Vaulting shaft: Slim column on a → pier or wall supporting → transverse arches, → ribs or → archivolts; mostly half or three-quarter round.

Westwork: The west end of a church, consisting of mostly free-standing structures (tower, entrance hall, → transept).

Included in this bibliography are only the more recent publications giving an overview of the Gothic and information about the current state of research. Each of the publications contains extensive lists of further reading.

Anderson, William: *The Rise of the Gothic*, London, 1985.

Aubert, Marcel: *Hochgotik*, Baden-Baden, 1963.

Binding, Günther: *Architektonische Formenlehre*, 4th ed., rev. and compl., Darmstadt, 1998.

Binding, Günther: *Maßwerk*, Darmstadt, 1989.

Binding, Günther: *Baubetrieb im Mittelalter*, Darmstadt, 1993.

Binding, Günther: *Beiträge zum Gotik-Verständnis*, 2nd ed., Cologne, 1996.

Binding, Günther: *Der früh- und hochmittelalterliche Bauherr als sapiens architectus*, 2nd ed., Darmstadt, 1998.

Bony, Jean: *French Gothic Architecture of the 12th and 13th Century*, Berkeley, 1983.

Branner, Robert: *Burgundian Gothic Architecture*, London, 1960.

Duby, Georges: *Die Kunst des Mittelalters. Das Europa der Kathedralen 1140–1280*, Geneva, 1985 (1st ed., 1966).

Erlande-Brandenburg, Alain: *Triumph der Gotik 1260–1380*, Munich, 1988 (Universum der Kunst, 34; *La conquête de l'Europe*, Paris, 1987).

Erlande-Brandenburg, Alain: *Quand les cathédrales étaient peintes*, Paris, 1993.

Frankl, Paul: *The Gothic. Literary Sources and Interpretations through Eight Centuries*, Princeton, 1960.

Frankl, Paul: *Gothic Architecture*, Harmondsworth, 1962 (Pelican History of Art).

Franz, H. Gerhard: *Spätromanik und Frühgotik*, Baden-Baden, 1969.

Grodecki, Louis: *Architektur der Gotik*, Stuttgart / Milan, 1976 (Weltgeschichte der Architektur, ed. Pier Luigi Nervi); 2nd ed., Stuttgart, 1986.

Gross, Werner: *Gotik und Spätgotik*, Frankfurt a. M., 1969 (Epochen der Architektur).

Harvey, John: *The Gothic World, 1100–1600*, London, New York, Toronto, 1950.

Harvey, John: *The Master Builders. Architecture in the Middle Ages*, New York, 1971.

Henderson, George: *Gothic*, Harmondsworth, 1967.

Jantzen, Hans: *Kunst der Gotik*, Hamburg, 1957 (new ed. by Hans-Joachim Kunst, Berlin, 1987).

Jantzen, Hans: *Die Gotik des Abendlandes*, Cologne, 1962.

Kidson, Peter and Peter Murray: *A History of English Architecture*, London et. al., 1962.

Kimpel, Dieter and Robert Suckale: *Die gotische Architektur in Frankreich 1130–1270*, Munich, 1985.

Kowa, Günter: *Architektur der Englischen Gotik*, Cologne, 1990.

Mâle, Émile: *Die Gotik. Kirchliche Kunst des XIII. Jahrhunderts in Frankreich*, Stuttgart / Zurich, 1986 (*L'art religieux du XIIIe siècle en France. Études sur l'iconographie du Moyen Age et sur ses sources d'inspiration*, Paris, 1958).

Michler, Jürgen: 'Über die Farbfassung hochgotischer Sakralräume', in: *Wallraf-Richartz-Jahrbuch*, 39, 1977, pp. 29–64.

Michler, Jürgen: *Die Elisabethkirche zu Marburg in ihrer ursprünglichen Farbigkeit*, Marburg, 1984.

Nußbaum, Norbert: *Deutsche Kirchenbaukunst der Gotik*, 2nd ed., Darmstadt, 1994.

Recht, Roland (ed.): *Les bâtisseurs des cathédrales gothiques*, Strasbourg, 1989.

Sauerländer, Willibald: *Das Jahrhundert der großen Kathedralen 1140–1260*, Munich, 1990 (Universum der Kunst, 36; *Le grand siècle des cathédrales*, Paris, 1989).

Sedlmayr, Hans: *Die Entstehung der Kathedrale*, Zurich, 1950; 2nd ed., Graz, 1976.

Seeger, Ulrike: *Zisterzienser und Gotikrezeption. Die Bautätigkeit des Babenbergers Leopold VI. in Lilienfeld und Klosterneuburg*, Munich / Berlin, 1997.

Simson, Otto von: *The Gothic Cathedral*, New York, 1956.

Simson, Otto von: *Das hohe Mittelalter*, Berlin, 1972 (Propyläen Kunstgeschichte 6).

Swaan, Wim: *The Gothic Cathedral*, London, 1969 (special ed., 1996).

Ullmann, Ernst: *Die Welt der gotischen Kathedrale*, Berlin, 1981.

Wagner-Rieger, Renate: *Die italienische Baukunst zu Beginn der Gotik*, 2 vols., Graz / Cologne, 1956, 1957.

INDEX – Persons

ACKNOWLEDGEMENTS AND CREDITS

I am indebted to the many authors whose works I have consulted – their names are listed in the bibliography. Julia Benthien, Britta Bommert and Maria Spitz helped in many ways during the preparation of the manuscript. And my colleague, Professor Dr Andreas Speer at the Thomas Institute of the University of Cologne provided welcome advice and ideas. I would also like to thank the editors, Dr Angela Pfotenhauer, Dr Susanne Klinkhamels, Caroline Keller and Dr Nicola Senger, for their kind and professional support, in particular with respect to meeting my specific requirements in terms of photographs; working with them was a great pleasure.

The majority of the photographs illustrating this book have been taken by Uwe Dettmar.

In addition, a series of documents were helpfully provided by various institutions and photographers, in particular:

Pages 5 and 28: © Österreichische Nationalbibliothek
Pages 6, 218, 219, 220, and 221: © Anne and Henri Stierlin
Pages 12, 13, 36, 62–63, 82, 91, 96, 97, 114, 115, 117, 127, 187, 188, 190, 191, 192–193, 194, 195, 196, 197, 198, 199, 202, 203, 205, 206, 207, 209, 210, 211, and 215: © Florian Monheim
Pages 17, 55, 70, 71, and 213: © Günther Binding
Page 24: © Giraudon
Page 58: © Bibliothèque municipale de Toulouse
Pages 60 and 61: © The Board of Trinity College Dublin
Page 73 left: © Bernisches Historisches Museum, Bern
Page 73 right: © CRDP Clermont-Ferrand, France
Pages 75 and 77: © The Pierpont Morgan Library / Art Resource, NY
Pages 78 and 79: © Bibliothèque nationale de France
Page 118: © Manfred Schuller, Bauforschung Universität Bamberg
Page 129: © Photo RMN – Daniel Arnaudet
Pages 200, 201, 204, and 208: © Florian Monheim / Roman von Götz
Pages 214 and 222: © Claude Huber
Page 223: © Heinz Götze
Page 224: © Editoriale Jaca Book, Milan

Finally, the plans were created especially for this book by Alberto Berengo Gardin: Pages 8, 8–9, 14, 88, 95, 119, 146, 154, 157, 161, 166, 171, 197, 199, 210, 213, 223, and 232.

ALL 40 TITLES AT A GLANCE

Each book: US$ 29.99 | £ 16.99 | CDN$ 39.95

"... a truly remarkable publishing event in architecture."
The Architectural Review
London

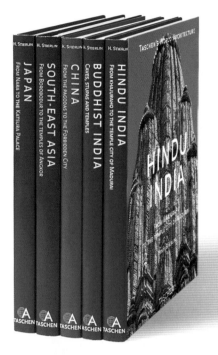

▶ Collect 40 volumes of TASCHEN'S WORLD ARCHITECTURE in eight years (1996–2003) and build up a complete panorama of world architecture from the earliest buildings of Mesopotamia to the latest contemporary projects.

▶ The series is grouped into five-volume units, each devoted to the architectural development of a major civilisation, and introducing the reader to many new and unfamiliar worlds.

▶ Each volume covers a complex architectural era and is written so vividly that most readers will feel the urge to go out and discover these magnificent buildings for themselves.

TASCHEN'S WORLD ARCHITECTURE

"An excellently produced, in-formative guide to the history of architecture. Accessible to everyone."
Architektur Aktuell, Vienna

"This is by far the most compre-hensive review of recent years."
Frankfurter Rundschau, Frankfurt

"A successful debut of a very promising series."
Architektur & Wohnen, Hamburg, on *Islam from Baghdad to Cordoba*

"...each theme is presented in a very interesting, lively style... it makes you want to set off straight away to see everything with your own eyes."
Baumeister, Munich, on *The Roman Empire*

▶ TASCHEN'S WORLD ARCHITECTURE presents 6000 years of architectural history in 40 volumes.

▶ Each volume is a detailed and author-itative study of one specific era.

▶ The whole series provides a compre-hensive survey of architecture from antiquity to the present day. Five volumes will be published each year.

▶ TASCHEN'S WORLD ARCHITECTURE is a must for all lovers of architecture and travel.

▶ Renowned photographers have travelled the world for this series, presenting more than 12000 photographs of famous and lesser-known buildings.

▶ Expert authors guide the reader through TASCHEN'S WORLD ARCHI-TECTURE with exciting, scientifically well-founded texts that place architec-ture within the cultural, political and social context of each era.

▶ The elegant, modern design and the clear, visually striking layout guide the reader through the historical and contemporary world of architecture.

▶ Influential architectural theories, typical stylistic features and specific construction techniques are separately explained on eye-catching pages.

▶ Each volume includes between 40 and 50 maps, plans and structural drawings based on the latest scholarly findings and are produced for this series using state-of-the-art computer technology.

▶ The appendix contains clear chronolo-gical tables, giving an instant overview of the correlation between the histor-ical events and architecture of any given civilisation.

▶ A detailed glossary clearly explains architectural terms.

▶ An index of names and places ensures quick and easy reference to specific buildings and people.

▶ Each book contains 240 pages with some 300 color illustrations on high-quality art paper. 240 x 300 mm, hardcover with dust jacket.

Each book: US$ 29.99 | £ 16.99 | CDN$ 39.95